Carol Haag
June 24th 1985
4825 N.W. 253rd
Hillsboro, OR
97124

American Style

FLOWER ARRANGING

Peter B. Pfahl

**Professor Emeritus of Floriculture
Pennsylvania State University**

Elwood W. Kalin

**Professor of Floriculture
Washington State University**

Prentice-Hall, Inc., Englewood Cliffs, NJ 07632

Library of Congress Catologing in Publication Data

Pfahl, Peter Blair, (date)
    American style flower arranging.

    Includes index.
    1. Flower arrangement.   2. Flower arrangement—
United States.   I. Kalin, Elwood W.   II. Title.
SB449. P45   745.92'24   81-10739
ISBN 0-13-029538-8   AACR2

Cover Photo: A typical American symmetrical flower arrangement. (Courtesy FTDA.)

© 1982 by Prentice-Hall, Inc., Englewood Cliffs, N.J. 07632

Printed in the United States of America

10 9 8 7 6 5 4 3

Editorial/production supervision
  and interior design by Leslie I. Nadell
Page layout by Peter Ticola
Cover design by Edsal Enterprise
Manufacturing buyer: John Hall

PRENTICE-HALL INTERNATIONAL, INC., *London*
PRENTICE-HALL OF AUSTRALIA PTY. LIMITED, *Sydney*
PRENTICE-HALL OF CANADA, LTD., *Toronto*
PRENTICE-HALL OF INDIA PRIVATE LIMITED, *New Delhi*
PRENTICE-HALL OF JAPAN, INC., *Tokyo*
PRENTICE-HALL OF SOUTHEAST ASIA PTE. LTD., *Singapore*
WHITEHALL BOOKS LIMITED, *Wellington, New Zealand*

Dedicated to:

EDYTHE and FRANCES
Whose help, encouragement and understanding
made this book possible

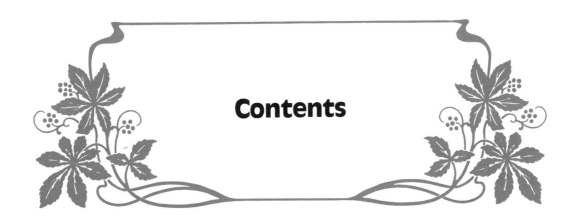

Contents

Contents

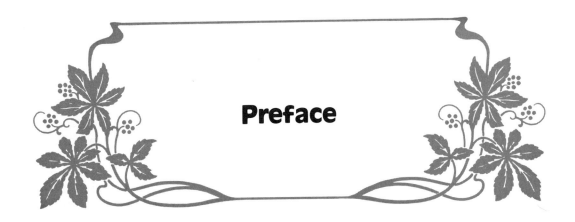

Preface

There are many books available on flower arranging. So, why a new one? Because this particular book discusses **American** flower arrangements, which are a challenging combination of arrangements from the Orient and Europe that serve as the basis for the traditional flower arrangements in America today. They are a combination of *line, mass,* and *line-mass* arrangements.

Anyone can learn to make a flower arrangement that is aesthetically pleasing. What is needed is the desire to create something beautiful and a willingness to study and practice.

The challenging and rewarding art of flower arranging provides the floral artist with numerous personal and general benefits. Flowers and flower arranging offers the arranger more enjoyment from his or her home surroundings; a degree of self-satisfaction; fulfillment of a creative need; a facet of horticultural therapy; and an accomplishment of discovering and using a greater utility of both individual blossoms and flowers as a group once they are arranged.

The authors present the steps to creative flower arranging in a logical sequence that results in a flower arrangement both pleasing to the eye and artistically correct. The book emphasizes the American style of flower arranging beginning with an examination of its historical background; it then describes the principles and steps underlying today's contemporary American arrangements, and suggests some ideas on designs for the future.

American Style Flower Arranging will be a valuable tool for students in colleges and universities, two-year agricultural colleges, vocational-training schools, and floral design schools. In teaching, it is wise to remember that a laboratory should be incorporated with the course. Practice of what is learned in this book is an essential ingredient for successful flower arranging. The text will also be useful to garden club men and women who are interested in making flower arrangements for use in the home, flower shows, or other garden club activities as well as to anyone interested in flowers and the creation of flower arrangements.

People will find *American Style Flower Arranging* challenging and interesting and a source for both knowledge and increased understanding. Once read, both young and old will probably want to try their hands at arranging flowers.

ACKNOWLEDGEMENTS

We wish to thank FTDA, Teleflora, Inc., the National Council of State Garden Clubs, Jennifer Brown, Kathy Kanouse Farr, John Francis (editing manuscript), and flower arrangers of the National Council for their help with the pictures, drawings, editing, and assemblage of this book.

Peter B. Pfahl
State College, Pennsylvania

Elwood W. Kalin
Pullman, Washington

part
I

THE
BEGINNING

1

The Challenges of Flower Arranging

Flower arranging is the art of arranging flowers and/or other plant materials in a container in a pleasing manner following basic principles of design. Flower arranging combines the disciplines and skills of many of the major art forms. Like a painter, the flower arranger deals in shapes, color, balance, and proportion. The flower arranger's colors are not paints on a palette, but the glowing colors of nature. The lines are not of ink or charcoal, but the living lines of stems and branches.

Like a sculptor, the flower arranger deals with masses and spaces, light and shadow, the emotions evoked by three-dimensional forms. But the flower arranger does not need the strength and time to hammer stone or weld metal; he deals not with the textures of iron or marble, but the textures of bark, fronds, and petals.

In many ways, a flower arranger is like a composer of music. Unordered notes are just noise, but when collected and arranged, they form music. And those same notes can be collected in an infinite number of ways to produce all kinds of music. So it is with the flower arranger; like the individual notes of music, the individual flowers, branches, and leaves await their gathering and arrangement. As the musical composer has his instruments, rhythms, and harmonies to work with, so the flower arranger has his shapes, containers, and designs with which to fashion his composition, his unified visual "song." And like a piece of music, the flower arrangement can be ornate or simple, modest or grandiose, flamboyant or subdued, and designed either for an audience of thousands or for a single friend (Figure 1.1).

Figure 1.1 Roses always say "Welcome!" (Courtesy Teleflora, Inc.)

And, like all artistic forms, you can never come to the end of it; the more you learn about flower arranging, the more you can explore, the farther you can travel. The larger the island of knowledge, the longer the shoreline of wonder.

As with all arts, knowledge and discipline are needed for flower arranging. You will need to know the principles of design and color. You will have to practice, experiment, test concepts, and make mistakes. Flower arrangers have the advantage of working with materials that are themselves works of art in nature. Flowers, leaves, and branches already have their own inherent beauty and complexity. On the other hand, the materials are sometimes difficult to manipulate and sometimes resist being used together.

The more you work with flowers, the more observant you will become, the more conscious of textures, colors, and shapes. Each combination and arrangement you try will suggest others; you will find your visual horizons expanding.

Flower arranging is an immediate art form. Your creations are fragile and transient. An arrangement may last only a few days, but the materials for a new one are as close as your garden. Imagine a marble statue beside a bowl of flowers. Each day the flowers are changed, the statue remains the same. The block of marble came from far away and was laboriously carved and shaped, the flowers grow beside it. The statue lasts for centuries, the flowers are changed each day. And as the years pass, the statue and the ever-changing flowers remain together, neither "superior" to the other, examples of change and permanence, the two faces of eternity.

THE AMERICAN STYLE OF FLOWER ARRANGING

American flower arranging has evolved by borrowing, combining, and building upon the principles of Japanese and European flower arranging. The American style incorporates both the strong line and form stressed by the Japanese and the mass styles of the Europeans. The three types of designs found in American flower arranging are *line, mass,* and *line–mass.* The *line–mass* style is most popular at present.

The Japanese confine their displays to specific areas as a matter of ritual and custom. Europeans use their arrangements primarily for religious functions or as gifts. In European homes, flowers are normally confined to the living room.

Americans place their flowers everywhere, in every room of the house, in every sort of business establishment. From a bathroom to a factory, no place is considered "inappropriate." And because they can be placed in such a wide variety of environments, the scope for arrangers is limitless.

Americans are surrounded by *designed* objects—cars, buildings, furniture, jewelry—and the designs in general are clean, sleek, "modern." This is reflected in the prevailing flower arranging styles which emphasize sleek, undecorated, modern containers.

Originality, individuality, and innovation have always been admired in America, and this is reflected in American flower arranging. Japanese and European arranging is more bound up with tradition; American arranging places greater emphasis on originality and distinctiveness, on experiments with untried combinations of plant materials, containers, and settings (Figure 1.2).

Figure 1.2 A contemporary arrangement of *camellias,* clipped palms, and variegated liriope. (Courtesy Marie L. Erwin, Sacramento, CA.)

2
History of Flower Arranging in the Orient

The floral artist needs to appreciate the history of flower arrangements, for it shows how present styles evolved from past traditions. Artists reach new heights by standing on the shoulders of those who have gone before (Figure 2.1).

Since the beginning of civilization, people have used flowers to beautify their surroundings, express their feelings, and commemorate important ceremonies. The ancient Egyptians used them to honor the pharaohs, welcome guests, decorate houses, and remember the dead. The most ancient legends talk of rich and ornate gardens.

Historical knowledge of flower arranging has come from many sources: paintings, sculpture, tombs, ceramics, music, books, poems, legends, tapestries, even kimonos and burial shrouds. Our richest source is the "flower pictures" of the 17th, 18th, and 19th centuries, which portrayed bouquets of flowers. The accuracy of these paintings is suspect—many times they show flowers that bloom in different seasons grouped together or vases that could not possibly contain the number of flowers that they do. The pictures reveal that the emphasis was on bouquets, which present individual flowers to their best advantage with little attention to their relation to each other. The paintings indicate that flower arranging, as we know it today, did not exist or existed in only the simplest ways. Our present-day *period arrangements* can only be adaptations of flower paintings to show the influence of a particular historical period, yet the flower paintings are a source of interesting ideas.

Figure 2.1 The ancient Asiatic aster (China aster) used in a pyramid design. (Courtesy Teleflora, Inc.)

CHINESE

The development of Oriental floral art through the centuries is inseparable from the history of the Oriental people, their customs, traditions, religions, and their unswerving love and appreciation of the beauties of nature. Floral styles also reflect the changes in art that accompany changes in cultures.

The Oriental country best known for its floral art is Japan, but the history of Japanese floral art cannot be understood without first examining its forerunner, Chinese floral art.

Oriental floral art was founded on religious principles, first Confucianism and then Buddhism. Floral art in early China was stimulated by the development of pottery and porcelain. Ceramics was highly developed in China and the vessels lent themselves to flower arranging. Ceramics, unlike bronze, ivory, and marble, were affordable by the general population and, consequently, the art of floral decoration spread among the common people. Flowers, plants, bulbs, and dwarfed trees became commonplace touches in Chinese houses. Courtyard gardens were developed as well, so that flowers and plants were always available for use in the house.

Flowers and plants became an integral part of Chinese life. They were placed on religious altars and household and temple shrines; they were written about by poets, painted by the famous Chinese masters, and worn by Chinese women in their hair. For hundreds of years, plant material has been used symbolically in China for seasonal decoration, celebrations, holidays, personal greetings and congratulations, and as an important facet of religion.

The Chinese never used flowers in the luxuriant, exuberant manner of the Europeans, who love large, colorful bouquets. The Chinese method of handling flowers is founded on symbolism, preservation of life, and appreciation of beauty. This results in a handling method which is restrained but never stylized. In Chinese floral art we see the subtle development of spatial relationships. The emphasis is on unity and rhythm.

The interpretation of Chinese flower arrangements deals with three important principles: the art of contemplation as practiced by the followers of Confucius, the principle of the preservation of life as taught by Buddhism, and the floral symbolism which has developed as a form of folklore.

Confucius taught that real enjoyment consists of simplicity and contemplation. A few flowers in a vase can describe the whole life history of a plant, as well as display the beauty of a perfect bloom.

In the 4th and 5th centuries, Buddhism began to become more influential. Temple priests during the time of Confucius promoted the use of flowers for religious ceremonies. Buddhists did the same.

Probably the most influential and important person in all the ancient arts of China was Hsieh Ho, a renowned painter. Ho lived during the 5th century A.D. He was a celebrated art critic and author, and published the *Six Canons* of the basic principles of painting. In addition to painting, these principles also applied to another facet of Chinese art, flower arranging. The six canons of the essential components of design have influenced Chinese artists ever since.

The first and most important canon is rhythmic vitality. Movement is the very life of Chinese art.

The second is organic structure or, literally, "bony structure." In Chinese painting, "bone" is a line which is continuous and strong from the beginning to the end.

The third is conformity with nature. The essential characteristics should be shown and all superfluous details avoided.

The fourth is appropriate coloring. The color should be in keeping with the true nature of the object. The color of the different parts should be harmonious with one another and with the surroundings.

The fifth is planning the design and composition.

The final principle is the transmitting of the design. The style of a composition should convey to the viewer the emotions and ideas of the composer.

The six canons, though not literally followed at all times, became nevertheless the basic principles of Chinese art. These principles were also applied to floral art in Japan. The rules followed today by the various schools of flower arrangement in Japan all derive from Hsieh Ho's *Six Canons* of nearly 1500 years ago.

From the earliest days, the Chinese people expressed devotion to their ancestors by offering flowers and branches. This custom was introduced in Japan in the 6th century by the Chinese priests who brought Buddhism to Japan. These missionary priests brought with them beautiful T'ang ceremonial bronze vases, which they used for floral offerings. As the new religion spread, many temples were built and altar vessels were adopted from Chinese originals. The priests not only evolved a system of arranging flowers, but they developed many ways of prolonging the life of flowering material. They also furthered the symbolic lore associated with flowers. These early altar arrangements made by the priests were known as *shin-no-hana*. Each one was arranged around a central stem or branch called *shin*, a term frequently used in Japanese flower arranging. The flowers were originally offered in a very primitive manner, but as time passed more care and concern was shown in the votive placement of the flowers.

JAPANESE

Rikka (Rikkwa)

The Chinese floral art evolved in Japan into a highly stylized and formal temple art called *Rikka* or *Rikkwa*. Prince Shotoku (573-621 A.D.), a popular ruler in Japan distinguished for his democratic ideas, caused a widespread conversion of the Japanese to Buddhism. As a result, Rikka became a popular design style in which people could take the initiative when applying to their home decorations.

Rikka means *standing flowers* and describes arrangements made of evergreens, foliage, flowers, and, often, bare branches. The early Rikka arrangements made by the priests were very large and tall and sometimes took days to construct. Many were 6 feet tall, and some were recorded as large as 15 feet tall and 12 feet wide.

Initially, their composition consisted of seven branches, but modifications brought the number up to nine and, subsequently, to eleven. One of the underlying ideas of these arrangements was that a natural landscape should be represented in its entirety, not so much in the placing as in the combination of materials selected. The Rikka floral art is a formalized style of design that builds around a dominant tall piece of plant material, very often a part of a tree, placed in the center of the container. Branches of

Figure 2.2 *Rikkwa* or temple arrangement. (Courtesy Kathy Kanouse Farr.)

different kinds of plant material are then placed as if growing with exact preciseness from the main stalk (Figure 2.2).

Ikenobo (Ikebana)

In the latter part of the 7th century, a famous Japanese scholar named Ono-no-Imoko made three trips to China to study philosophy, government, and art. Upon his return he was appointed master of the Rokkakudo Temple of Kyoto. While living on the temple grounds near a lake, he arranged flowers for the altar of the temple in memory of his patron. As he arranged the flowers, he formulated certain rules for arranging that resulted in the founding of the first school in Japan for floral art. It became known as *Ikenobo*, which means *priest by the lake*. The school is still in existence today and many other schools have branched off from it. The different schools of flower arrangement have used the same fundamental principles and traditions. The main differences have been in the kinds of containers and flower holders they are permitted to use.

Figure 2.3 An excellent example of *Ikebana* in the *Gyo* (semi-formal) style. (Courtesy Kathy Kanouse Farr.)

Ikenobo, a formalized type of an arrangement, consists of three triangular groups: an upright central group, an intermediate group leaning away from the upright structure, and an inverted triangle group that leans away from the central group on the opposite side of the intermediate group.

Ikenobo became so popular that it gave root to the style of Japanese floral art now referred to as *Ikebana*. At the present time, the two words are often used interchangeably, with Ikebana now the preferred term.

Ikebana is based upon principles of dominance, proportion, balance, and rhythm to symbolize philosophical concepts of Buddhism. Emphasis is on line, symmetry, depth, and sharp silhouettes; flowers and colors are secondary (Figures 2.3 and 2.4).

With the exception of Rikka, the many Japanese schools past and present, while practicing their own interpretations of the basic principles of Japanese flower art, all emphasize asymmetrical balance, with the basic form of design being triangular. In creating the triangle configuration, the three elements of *heaven, man,* and *earth* are fundamental. The *heaven*

(Shin, Shu, Ten) line is the tallest and is placed vertically. It is at least one and one-half times the height of the container (or the breadth of a low dish). The height of each line is measured from its tip in a straight line to the rim of a vase or to the water of a low dish. A gentle curve is often forced into the heaven line if it did not have one to begin with, and the tip of the branch or flower must appear directly over the spot where the stem comes out of the water in order to gain ideal balance.

The *man* (Soe, Hikae, Chi) line is two-thirds or sometimes one-half the height of the heaven line. It is also vertical and placed to either side.

The *earth* (Tai, Negime, Jin) line is one-third or sometimes one-fourth the height of the principle heaven line and is on the opposite side of the main line. It is placed in a more horizontal position. Intermediate lines, subordinate to the three main elements, are called *Chukkan*.

With such rigid rules, it would seem that these trilinear arrangements might be tiresomely alike. Actually, great variation is possible within the confines of a triangle when you consider the various heights of the arrange-

Figure 2.4 A semi-formal *Ikebana* using cypress. (Courtesy Kathy Kanouse Farr.)

ments, the various proportions of the triangle, and of course the infinite variety in plant material.

The art of flower arranging developed very slowly in Japan and the many schools now so popular did not come into existence until the end of the 15th century. From the 15th to the 17th centuries, the Japanese masters slowly evolved their own characteristic proportions and rhythm of lines in the Ikebana style. One of the first improvements in Ikebana was made when Sen no Rikyu, a priest and famous tea master, became the head of the Senke school early in the 16th century. Because the costly bronze and brass containers normally used could only be afforded by the wealthy, Sen no Rikyu introduced containers made of bamboo which were easily affordable by all classes.

Yoshimasa (1436-1490 A.D.), eighth Shogun of the Ashikaga Dynasty and a patron of the arts, was the greatest promoter of *Cha-no-yu*, the tea ceremony; *Ikebana*, the flower arrangement; and *Koawase*, the incense ceremony. These types of arrangements, often called the *Seika* or classical style, were created about 1450. Yoshimasa had great influence on the social and artistic development of his country. He introduced the design for small houses which included the now typical household religious shrine or built-in alcove called the *tokonoma*, in which a hanging scroll painting, a flower arrangement, and sometimes an art object were placed.

Yoshimasa said that flowers presented on ceremonial occasions or placed as offerings before the gods should not be offered loosely but should represent time and thought. From this pronouncement, the rules for Ikebana began to be formulated. Yoshimasa also had much to do with the perfection of the tea ceremony *Chan-no-yu*. It became an integral part of Japanese life and influenced the architecture of the home, design of the garden, and the development of painting, as well as the creation of tea-drinking vessels.

The celebrated painter Soami, a contemporary and friend of Yoshimasa, is given credit for the inspiration and translocation of Yoshimasa's idea of time and thought for floral offerings into rules and symbolism. Soami conceived the idea of representing the three elements of heaven, man, and earth (ten-chi-jin) in Japanese floral art. These three main elements are the principles upon which Japanese floral art has been developed and are very evident to the present time.

In the past, three main types of Ikenobo (Ikebana) arrangements were made. All were based on the three elements heaven, man, and earth. The tall and formal types which made use of flowers just as they grew naturally were called *Shin* (formal). No artificial bending or coaxing of curves was used, although there was pruning of excess material. The Shin type of arrangement used mostly upright vases of bronze or pottery.

A semi-formal classification called *Gyo* was made up of gently curving stems placed in broader, upright vases of medium height, such as a usubata or a basket.

The *So* (informal) style of arrangement had sweeping lines, produced by forced bending, and took on an informality and a horizontal emphasis. Containers for this style varied, and included low bronze or pottery receptacles called *suibans*, bamboo cylinders (some double- or triple-tiered), pottery "boats," hanging bamboo "boats," "moons," and gourds.

Nageire

The Rikka and Ikebana styles of Japanese flower arranging were classical and formal in concept. Coexisting with them was a more naturalistic, informal style called *Nageire* or *thrown in* style, which was practiced by people outside religious circles. This seemingly casual mode of flower arrangement became well-known in the 16th century, growing in popularity along with the tea ceremony. The simplicity of room decoration, both in public tea houses and in private homes, called for correspondingly simple flower arrangements (Figure 2.5). The seemingly artless arrangements possessed great subtlety and a high degree of skill was

Figure 2.5 A *Nageire* arrangement of columbine. (Courtesy Kathy Kanouse Farr.)

required to create the "casual" effects. Vases only, never low dishes, were used in the Nageire style. This style grew in popularity from the 16th through the 19th centuries and rivaled the popularity of the classical Ikebana style.

Moribana

Western influence has been responsible, since the beginning of the 20th century, for the development of a new kind of arrangement known as *Moribana*, which is an adaptation of older styles without specific symbolism. The Moribana style is purely naturalistic. It was developed for use in homes built and furnished in the Western manner and makes use of Western flowers. Moribana has found two modes of expression: the landscape scene, made up of carefully selected branches and a few flowers, and the grouping of cut flowers alone. Low dishes are used. Branches represent trees, and rocks and moss represent islands or land and are set in open water areas. Materials such as minor bulbs or low growing plants are placed in the fore-

Figure 2.6 A *Moribana* arrangement of cherry branches. (Courtesy Kathy Kanouse Farr.)

ground. Moribana compositons are created differently in spring, summer, autumn, and winter (Figure 2.6).

These are some general characteristics of Japanese flower arrangements (Figure 2.7):

1. Each flower's characteristic beauty is emphasized.

2. Flowers and plant materials are considered to show their best advantage when placed in a design rather than in their natural environment.

3. The arrangement is three-dimensional.

4. Asymmetrical balance in the trilinear form is used.

5. Proportional dimensions of long, medium, and short stems are roughly 3:2:1.

6. Design consists of a three-stem, five-stem, seven-stem, or nine-stem framework, with other plant material or filler completing the design.

7. In each arrangement, there is a dominant material, an intermediate material, and a subordinate material.

Figure 2.7 *Free Style,* an intriguing arrangement in the Japanese manner, combining *camellias* and *aspidistra.* (Courtesy Mrs. Paul Kincaid, Gastonia, NC.)

8. Each arrangement has a definite focal point of flowers, leaves, and/or branches.

9. Foliage which occurs naturally with the flowers is most often used.

10. All of the material emerges from the container at one point to give the appearance of the arrangement being more natural, as if it were a single tree or branch.

11. The arrangements are designed to look best from the front, since they must fit into small alcoves or *Tokonoma*.

12. Completed arrangements are frequently placed on stands or bases that form a part of the design.

13. Arrangements usually use flowers and branches in varying stages of maturity from tight bud to open development.

14. The use of branches and twigs, with or without flowers, is emphasized because of the importance of form, material, and strong line.

3
History of Flower Arranging in the Mediterranean and Europe

The art of any period of civilization reflects the tastes and ideas of that time and place. In general, Mediterranean and European flower arrangements have emphasized mass and color, compared to the Japanese emphasis on line. In early Mediterranean and European history, flowers were used mainly for religious and festive occasions, and the arrangements were quite large and ornate. They also had some degree of symbolism since certain flowers were often associated with a specific god or rite. Smaller floral pieces were sometimes used for home decorations. People wore wreaths and garlands.

As time passed, European flower arrangers tried to "bring the garden into the house." As many different types of flowers and colors were combined as could be found in their beautiful gardens.

EGYPTIAN PERIOD (2800-28 B.C.)*

The use of flowers was a highly developed aspect of the culture of ancient Egypt. Stacked bowls of flowers, or fruit and flowers, were used as temple offerings and as banquet table decorations. Flowers and foliage were formed into head wreaths, garlands, or collars for guests. In processions, Egyptians

---

*The history of Mediterranean and European flower arranging has been divided into periods. Information on each period has been obtained from paintings, tombs, literature, tapestries, sculpture, bas-reliefs, jewelry, ceramics, and architecture.

carried ornate gold and silver vases filled with flowers, especially the sacred lotus blossoms.

Lotus, *acacia*, roses, water lilies, violets, Madonna lilies, narcissus, jasmine, and poppies were among the species grown and used as cut flowers. Ivy and lotus leaves were popular foliage materials.

Existing containers from ancient Egypt, on display in museums, include low bowls of glass, pottery, and bronze, some with built-in flower holders, and baskets and fruit dishes on pedestals like compotes of a later time.

Egyptian design emphasized clarity. Each flower and leaf, each form and color, stood out sharply. Ordered simplicity was desired, not casual confusion or complexity. A typical Egyptian design would consist of a single flower, with a bud or leaf on either side, repeated around the rim or side of a vase. Egyptian designs featured repetition and alternation. Blue and green segments might follow each other around a vase, or a line of alternating short and long stems.

GREEK (CLASSICAL) PERIOD (600-150 B.C.)

The Greeks did not arrange flowers in bowls or other containers as commonly as the Egyptians did. As a part of religious festivals or rituals, flowers were strewn on the ground or made into garlands and wreaths. Wreaths were placed on the brows of living heroes and statues. Garlands were sent as funeral flowers and grave decorations. Wreaths of flowers, fruit, and leaves were borne on trays at banquets. Garlands of fresh flowers decorated the tables on which baskets of fresh fruits and vegetables were placed. Lovers fashioned garlands of fragrant flowers, berries, seed pods, and leaves for each other.

Limited container arrangements were made in baskets, upright horns of plenty, or beautiful urns and offered in solemn rituals to gods in the temples. The arrangements were mostly of a symmetrical, triangular form. Buds were used as accents for the tips of the triangle, and small leaves were placed on each side of the neck of the container. Usually the flower arrangement was of one color or a limited combination of colors. White was frequently used since it was revered as a sign of purity.

The Greeks used the same flowers as the Egyptians, since the Egyptians sent their surplus to Greece and Rome. Locally, iris, thyme, and sweet marjoram were added, along with laurel and grape leaves.

ROMAN PERIOD (28 B.C.-325 A.D.)

The Romans created very little that was new in the use of flowers but retained the earlier customs of Greece. Low baskets of stacked fruits and flowers decorated banquet tables and guests were draped with floral wreaths and garlands. Cut roses were generously strewn about the floor and dropped from the ceiling in long garlands in a lavish display of color and fragrance.

Baskets and cornucopias were used for temple offerings but their designs were much heavier and less graceful than those of the Greeks.

EASTERN ROMAN EMPIRE PERIOD (BYZANTINE) (325-600 A.D.)

The portion of the Roman Empire in the vicinity of Byzantium on the Bosporus escaped the ravages of marauding tribes and the internal decay of the Western half. Evidence found in the church mosaics and tapestries shows a highly stylized, symmetrical technique of floral art. The compositions resembled elaborate Christmas trees. The arrangers used urns, chalices, and handled bowls of bronze, precious metals, glass, and semi-precious stones to build flower-decorated "trees." The compositions were inverted cones built along a central axis with symmetrical clusters of flowers or fruits. Tall containers were often filled with fans of tropical foliage, flanked by bunches of grapes or clusters of other fruit that dropped over the edge of the container. Perhaps this is the basis for today's practice of draping clusters of grapes over the edge of stemmed compotes.

The flowers were the same as those used in the Egyptian and early Roman periods, plus *anthuriums,* ginger, and other more tropical-type flowers.

MEDIEVAL PERIOD (475-1400 A.D.)

Very little is known about floral art between the fall of the western Roman Empire and the beginning of the Renaissance. From the 13th century, however, come tapestries, paintings, and manuscripts that tell of the use of tall vases of long-stemmed flowers as decorations for the numerous Gothic cathedrals of Europe. The arrangements were blended and subordinated to the appointments of the cathedral.

According to frescoes of the time, the most common style in cathedrals during the Gothic period consisted of a single tall stalk of lilies or roses in a handled urn or vase of precious metal placed on the floor before the altar. The stalk of flowers was two to three times as tall as the vase. The vase was circled at the top of the base with ferns, short-stemmed roses, or lilies-of-the-valley.

Some wreaths, garlands, and baskets were also presented as religious offerings. These usually contained roses, lilies, pinks, violets, and columbine, which were considered sacred to the Virgin.

RENAISSANCE PERIOD (ITALIAN)
(1400-1600 A.D.)

This period is often referred to as the *rebirth* or *reawakening*. It began in Italy and spread through the rest of Europe. The Renaissance was a time in history when interest in all the arts was revived. The period saw some of the world's great artists: Benvenuto Cellini (1500-1571), Hans Holbein (1460-1524), Luca della Robbia (1400?-1482), Sanzio Raphael (1483-1520), Sandro Botticelli (1447?-1510), Giovanni da Fiesole (Fra Angelico) (1387-1455), and Fra Filippo Lippi (1406?-1469). Cellini and Holbein created containers in metal reminiscent of the Byzantine era. Flower arranging in the early part of the period was characterized by large symmetrical arrangements made in urns, chalices, and bowls. The arrangements were set on a floor, window sill, or high shelf. Frequently, they were very tall arrangements, with lilies and roses in flared vases. The bowls and baskets contained symmetrical bouquets of light, airy, flowers—lilies-of-the-valley, pinks, and daisies (Figure 3.1).

The famous painter della Robbia is remembered for his symmetrical treatment of wreaths and garlands made of bright colored fruits, cones, berries, foliage, and flowers. These were the forerunners of our present-day Christmas wreaths and decorations.

As the Renaissance developed, so did the use of flowers. With the spread of printing in the early 16th century, people became more interested in gardening. The Italians soon became famous for their lovely gardens and their ability to grow magnificent flowers. They preferred to use them in large numbers and mixed kinds. An impression of richness and fullness was created by lavish use of flowers and fruits in containers full to overflowing.

One of the most popular containers was an urn made of heavy pottery, bronze, marble, or heavy Venetian glass. They also used bowls, jars, epergnes, pitchers, ewers*, and tall wide-lipped vases.

The arrangements were usually pyramidal, very full, and with bulging sides. Garlands of fruit were placed at the bottom of the container and trailed to the table top. Generally rich, velvety textures and warm colors with cool accents of blues and greens were preferred (Figure 3.2).

Paintings of the period show that a natural placement of flowers was being used for the first time. Tall stems rising gracefully from the containers, uncrowded and displaying their own natural form and color, were typical of the Renaissance period.

* A *ewer* is a pitcher having a wide spout and a handle.

Figure 3.1 A symmetrical massed arrangement matched with excellent accessories reminiscent of the Renaissance period. (Courtesy Teleflora, Inc.)

Figure 3.2 An epergne arrangement of flowers and fruit from the Italian Renaissance. (Courtesy Teleflora, Inc.)

FLEMISH PERIOD (BAROQUE) (1550-1760)

Toward the end of the Renaissance period in Italy, a new flamboyant and rhythmic style of flower painting began to spread throughout Europe as part of the baroque style of art, decoration, and architecture. The great Italian painter and sculptor Michelangelo Buonarroti (1475-1564) is considered to have given the period impetus by his extravagant decors. Flower arranging as an independent art form had not yet been established, and painters set the styles for floral design.

There were many flower painters in this period. The most prolific and popular lived in Holland and Flanders, hence the Dutch-Flemish period of influence. Included in this group were Jan Brueghel (1568-1625), Rembrandt van Rijn (1606-1669), Peter Rubens (1577-1640), and Hendrik van Balen (1575-1632).

A major English painter and engraver, William Hogarth (1697-1764), contributed a monumental expression to the art world. In a treatise published in 1753 entitled *Analysis of Beauty*, Hogarth described the configuration of a "lazy S" as the "line of beauty." "Straight is the line of duty, curved is the line of beauty." The Hogarthian curve is an asymmetrical rhythmic curve rendered in an upright or horizontal position (Figure 3.3).

The artists of the Renaissance created inspired flower paintings—and eventually flower arrangements—which were large, full to the point of overflowing, lavish, rhythmic, flamboyant, and carefully styled. Much care was given to the horticultural detail, selection, and placement of the flowers in an arrangement. Textures and colors were luxurious and rich. The arrangements were adorned with numerous accessories ranging from birds'

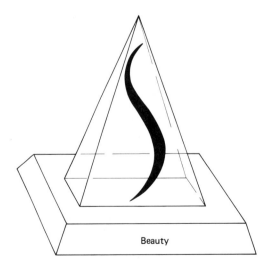

Beauty

Figure 3.3 Hogarth's *Line of Beauty*—"Straight is the line of duty; curved is the line of beauty." (Source: William Hogarth, *The Analysis of Beauty*, 1753.)

nests complete with eggs, butterflies, bees, and beetles to figurines, jewels, coins, fans, and fruits. In addition, for the first time in great houses, niches were especially designed to hold vases and urns of cut flowers. This permitted complete compositions of container, materials, and setting.

Flemish floral compositions used colors that were rich and dark—reds, dark blues, and purples—or subdued with occasional light areas. The containers were heavy urns, jugs, bowls, and vases in metal, glass, or stone. The bases were often narrow-necked.

Since the arrangements were large and heavy, the artists preferred to use the more massive flowers including lilies of all types, roses, hyacinths, tulips, narcissus, iris, callas, *gladiolus* sp., *delphinium*, lilacs, *scabiosa*, *salvia*, foxglove, carnations, garden pinks, hollyhock, and associated garden flowers and flowering shrubs. The favorite flower of the Flemish was the tulip.

FRENCH PERIOD (ROCOCO EMPIRE) (1715-1800)

Court life, beginning with King Louis XIV (1638-1715) in France, greatly influenced the art forms of Europe in the late 17th and 18th centuries. The tone was one of luxury, magnificence, and elegance, but the styles of flower painting and arranging were characterized by mild restraint. During the reign of King Louis XV (1710-1774) the rococo (rock and shell) style of art, an offshoot of the baroque, became predominant in France. Rococo art spread from France to other parts of Europe where it was exemplified by its frail, light, asymmetrical design and fanciful motifs of shells, scrolls, foliage, and flowers.

The ladies of the French court with their delicate, extravagant silk gowns and overdecorated feminine rooms made the rococo flower art more delicate in color and design than the baroque. Along with the larger, showier blossoms in a mass design, the courtly mode included compositions with frail and trailing vines such as honeysuckle, clematis, and morning glory, and slender-stemmed small blooms such as columbine, garden pinks, lilacs, larkspur, tulips, iris, narcissus, pansies, and flowering shrubs.

Instead of using the Hogarth lazy S curve of the baroque period, the rococo arrangements reflected the design motifs common in the architecture and furniture of the time—such as short, shell-like spiral curves and scrolls. The nodding flower heads curved on dainty stems gave rhythmic expression to the designs. Often a small number of flowers and buds were put in a fragile china vase or shell dish and placed on a side table in the ladies' boudoirs.

The more delicate treatment of floral materials was carried over into the types of containers used. Fine porcelain urns, classical alabaster vases, small shells, and leaf-shaped forms gilded and mounted on decorative bases were all adapted to floral art. China baskets, epergnes, wall pockets, cornucopias, fan-shaped china containers made of five separate bottlelike vases joined at the base and many other novelty types were created especially for cut flowers. China figurines were likewise designed as accessories for these elaborate floral designs. These containers and flowers required pale, delicate colors. Flower arrangements in the rococo period were more formal, more delicate and subtle in color, and more restrained in form than in the Flemish period although the French style was a direct offshoot from the Flemish and overlapped it.

GEORGIAN PERIOD (GREAT BRITAIN) (1715-1830)

In the 15th and 16th centuries, as fortresses gave way to individual houses and gardens, flowers came into the English home. The main concern at this time was fragrance; it was thought that a bouquet's perfume could rid the air of pestilence.

During the first half of the 18th century, flower artists of the Flemish period influenced the English form. The flower artists showed little concern for design, but simply crammed seasonal materials into wide-lipped, low urns. Sometimes bough pots (sturdy, oblong pots or jars) were filled with boughs and branches and placed in unused fireplaces during the summer.

During the last half of the 18th century and the first third of the 19th, a revival of classic architecture, decoration, and furnishings occurred in Great Britain, Europe, and America, partly in reaction to the baroque and rococo periods that preceded it. In France the decor was influenced by King Louis XVI (1754-1793). In Great Britain the cabinet makers, silversmiths, and ceramic makers set the style of flower art. Among the more famous of these artisans were the ceramist Josiah Wedgewood (1730-1795) and cabinet makers Thomas Sheraton (1751-1806), Robert Adams (1728-1792), James Adams (1730-1794), Thomas Chippendale (1718-1779), and George Heppelwhite (?-1786).

In the late Georgian period the flower arrangements were dignified, rich, definitely symmetrical. The finest types of flowers were combined with an elegant restraint in the choice and use of accessories. Line and design forms were vertical or horizontal, or combinations of these. A design often consisted of a broad base triangle. The vertical line was very strong and the horizontals were allowed to droop slightly to achieve gracefulness.

Flowers were placed in formal vases of porcelain, silver, or crystal in the drawing room. Silver candelabra and silver and glass containers were much used on dining tables. Other rooms of the house could contain a tightly arranged formal-feeling design in a Wedgewood container. Some containers were ingeniously designed with special holes and openings to hold the flowers in place and keep arrangements stiff and formal. The English are also given credit for creating the *nosegay*, or *tussy mussy*, and many historians suggest that the English were the first to use the centerpiece as we know it today.

Flower color was determined by room interior and, as Georgian homes favored pastel or medium values, the arrangements also favored these tints.

The favorite flower of English gardens was (and still is) the rose, and roses were used in every possible way. But the English garden is a treasure chest of flowers. The English used many of the flowers previously mentioned plus *primulas*, primroses, daffodils, Oriental poppies, hyacinths, iris, *delphinium, buddleia,* Madonna lilies, lavender, and heliotrope.

VICTORIAN PERIOD (GREAT BRITAIN)
(1800-1915)

Great Britain and its empire had a great influence on 19th century art forms. This included styles in architecture, art, clothing, and home furnishings. The Victorian era moved toward romanticism, cozy individualism, and comfort. There was a tendency to break away from classicism.

Victorian houses had large amounts of "gingerbread" wooden decoration for the many cupolas, porches, and ridges and eaves of the roof line. The ceilings of rooms were high, stairways were ornate, interior walls were covered with heavy, dark embossed wallpapers, and furniture tended toward plush- or velvet-covered overstuffed sofas and chairs and rosewood or mahogany tables and cabinets. Dark greens, rich reds, and browns were favored colors with figured rugs and carpets and somber paintings in large, highly ornamental gold frames. Dresses were heavily padded with leg-of-mutton sleeves, severely pinched-in waists, and long skirts with voluminous petticoats.

The flower arrangements were also profuse to the point of overflowing. Containers for Victorian flower arrangements were elaborately decorated and often flared. Urns and vases of alabaster were popular. Highly decorated and elaborately hand-painted vases of porcelain were highly prized. Epergnes of silver, pewter, and glass were filled to overflowing with popular garden flowers.

The standard array of English garden flowers was triangular or circular. Roses, especially the darker colors and whites, were very popular. Roses would be mixed with tulips, lilies, pansies, anemonies, dahlias, fuchsias, asters, bleeding hearts, and other garden flowers. Many of the flowers had short stems, so the height of the flowers in the arrangements was often no greater than the height of the container. Weeping or drooping lines of flowering vines, weeping willow, and bleeding heart were used to soften the hard line of the design. Victorian flower arrangers also included foliage and grasses in their arrangements for texture and contrast, and to complement the other materials used in the arrangement.

The tussy mussy originated in the Georgian period, but the ladies of the Victorian period perfected it. The tightly laced ladies of fashion assembled these small, fragrant bouquets with great care and carried them to social functions and church, where they sniffed them to revive themselves when overcome by sudden, but understandable, faintness.

The first European attempt to establish "rules" for flower design was made during the Victorian period. Many people seriously studied the techniques of flower arrangement. Women considered it an important decorative art, and during this era flower arranging achieved the status of an art. Authorities disagreed about the "rules" of flower arrangements, but all agreed that the form and color of flowers exerted a universal appeal.

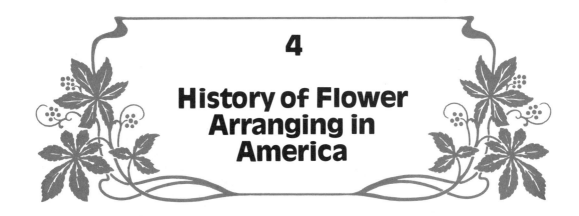

4
History of Flower Arranging in America

COLONIAL PERIOD (PILGRIM CENTURY) (1620-1775)

There are only sparse records of cut flowers in America from 1620 to the middle of the 18th century. It seems reasonable to assume that the Pilgrims of the Massachusetts Bay Colony considered the use of bouquets for house and personal adornment out of keeping with their tradition of austerity. We do know, however, that the Pilgrims brought with them seeds and roots of various plants which subsequently became established in the New World.

When church discipline loosened, the pioneers made bouquets of the flowers they brought with them and the wild flowers and grasses of their new home. The bouquets were in the restrained mode of Georgian England and of the Empire period of France. Since no room was available on the first sailing ships for luxuries such as vases, they used pitchers, bowls, pots, and jars of earthenware, pewter, or wood for containers.

Later, the more prosperous among the colonists of Virginia and Maryland and even the Quakers of Pennsylvania and Dutch New York brought vases, urns, epergnes, delft, floral bricks, pottery, posy holders, and stoneware from Holland and Great Britain to the New World. Oriental porcelain, glass, and silver began to be imported around 1700.

Simple garden flowers and dried materials were used in mass displays. Arrangements were both symmetrical and asymmetrical. Later during this period, the flower arrangements included flowers of pastel shades and many delicate flowers. Mixed bouquets of the Williamsburg tradition predominated.

These Williamsburg arrangements used the many varieties of flowers which grew in the gardens of Virginia during the 18th century. A typical flower arrangement of the Williamsburg period was the fan-shaped bouquet. Fine and feathery material was used around the edges in contrast to the solid masses of bloom at the center. Fresh flowers were used in the spring and summer with dried materials taking their place in the fall and winter.

The simple garden flowers of the period included anemones, lilies, roses, Dutch bulbs of all kinds, hollyhocks, *phlox*, sunflowers, violets, bachelor buttons, marigolds, pearly everlastings, strawflowers, daisies, pinks, carnations, and snapdragons.

VICTORIAN PERIOD (AMERICA) (1800-1920)

The Victorian period in America was very similar to that of England. Ornate containers of pottery, porcelain, silver, excellent quality earthenware, alabaster, and bronze urns, regular vases, and "flared" Victorian vases were filled to overflowing. The masses of flowers placed in the containers often appeared stiff and were what we would now call "old fashioned." White was popular but most arrangements were cool in color with emphasis on rich purples, magentas, and dark blues. The tussy mussy was also popular in America, especially in the "deep South" where pastels were preferred.

MODERN PERIOD (CONTEMPORARY)
(1910-PRESENT)

The new century ushered into America a transitional stage of flower design called the *New Art*. The Victorian influence began to fade after the death in 1901 of Queen Victoria. The stuffy, overcrowded Victorian decor began to be replaced by pastel colors, naturalism, and rhythmic forms.

Containers used for flowers came to be treated more as objects of art than as containers made only for flower arrangements. Glass vases in rich opalescent colors and unusual shapes, etched and decorated, were used. Dull-surfaced jars, bowls, and vases of pottery, French porcelain, heavy glass, and metal were freely decorated with birds and butterflies, or naturalistic floral patterns.

Fewer flowers were placed in these containers, primarily "bouquets" small enough to be held in the hand. The flower heights were short, usually only as tall as the vase, or slightly shorter.

During this period, the Western world began to become aware of the Japanese art of *line arrangements*. Branches of flowering shrubs and other woody and viney materials were placed in low dishes and Oriental bowls. These first arrangements did not always show good design technique, but they were the first Japanese influences on Western flower arranging.

With the end of World War I in 1918, the art of flower arranging began to spread quickly. America moved into an era of prosperity and "good times." Flower gardening again became popular, and greenhouse flower production was rapidly expanding. The horticulture shows began to include arrangement classes along with specimen displays. Flower arrangement teachers, often associated with the Federated Garden Clubs of America and The Garden Club of America, began to develop formal techniques and artistic elements and principles of design in flower arranging. Knowledgeable and experienced arrangers began writing books about raising garden flowers and flower arranging. Probably the most influential factor in advancing flower arrangement in this country has been the National Council of State Garden Clubs, with its yearbooks and other publications, and its development of judging schools and trained judges.

Flower arranging instructors began to disseminate the fundamental design principles, especially balance, scale and rhythm. These artists combined the elements of design in line and form of Japanese flower arranging with their own knowledge of the mass design of Europe and early America.

The contemporary American style began to evolve toward a pleasing combination of European mass with Oriental line. Today, American flower arrangers can explore and draw upon three traditions: the European world of mass design, the Oriental world of line design, and the American world of line-mass, a combination of the two. The American style of flower arrangement stresses clear-cut designs and plant forms, originality, and freedom of expression (Figure 4.1).

Mass Arrangements

Mass arrangements may utilize any of the basic geometrical forms: cylinder, pyramid, cone, sphere, or ovoid. The main requirement is that the entire area be filled with flowers and plant materials. This is not the profuse overflowing design of Europe, yet it creates the feeling of abundance. The composition of today has a definite color harmony, a segregation of color with gradual transition from one to the other, good symmetrical or asymmetrical balance, a strong focal point of massed plant material, less dense material to give graceful height and breadth, and emphasis on repetition, contrast, and texture. The containers should be substantial to hold the material easily and give a feeling of adequate support. Large flowers may be used in conjunction with lighter and airy blooms for contrast and texture.

Figure 4.1 Restrained usage of foliage for a fantasy arrangement of the 20th century (American). (Courtesy Teleflora, Inc.)

Line Arrangements

Line arrangements, quite naturally, are influenced by the Japanese styles. The contemporary line arrangement of today is less rigid and more free, giving modern artists an opportunity to explore the natural beauty of the plant materials instead of forcing them to obey rigid rules. Visually, a line arrangement is a floral design created entirely of lines and silhouettes of individual leaves and/or flowers. These, and the voids between and around them, form the design. Obviously, the arrangement contains less plant material and the voids take on greater significance. A symmetrically-balanced line arrangement is frequently constructed around a central figurine or other accessory as the focal point. The figurine may suggest the type of plant material to be used around it. Asymmetrical designs are more popular because they provide the artist with more freedom of expression. The choice of a heavy or light branch, vine, or thin-stemmed flower can change the rhythm of a design. The most popular basic forms are the lazy S Hogarth curve and the crescent. However, a spiral, a horizontal line or curve, and the L or V forms are also popular. The most obvious requirement is that the arrangement have a clean-cut design.

Line-Mass Arrangements

It is sometimes difficult to tell where the line arrangement leaves off and the line-mass begins, but in general we can say that when even a small amount of plant material is massed to form the focal point, the arrangement has become line-mass.

As previously mentioned, Japanese floral art has given great impetus to the now stylized conventional American line-mass design. This classic design has the following characteristics: clean-cut, sculptural design, with equal emphasis in the skeletal pattern of lines which determine the general shape of the arrangement, the voids between the lines and other plant forms, and the massed materials which give it weight, focus, and depth.

In line-mass arrangements the line portion is built into the design with branches, stems, or a series of blooms or leaves, usually of the steeple type, which creates a visual path to lead the eye from one point of interest to another. These lines and the voids they create are the skeletal pattern of the design. The mass portion is usually placed low and to the center of the design and along the main line axis or axes. The mass is heavier toward the center and thins out toward the outer edges of the arrangement. The plant materials should be repeated in form and color throughout the arrangement.

The basic form can be any common geometric figure such as a pyramid, cone, sphere, ellipsoid, cylinder, cube, or a modification or combination of these. The pyramid is the source of any triangular form. The partial sphere, crescent, or Hogarth curve are all derived from the sphere (Figure 4.2).

Containers for line-mass arrangements can be any traditional receptacle: urns, vases, bowls, and flat dishes made of glass, silver, pottery, earthenware, porcelain, bronze, etc. In addition, the modern era of plastics and stainless steel opens an unlimited choice of new containers. The opportunity for originality and freedom of expression presents endless possibilities for containers, from a hollowed-out pumpkin to a buggy wheel hub, from a thimble or half a walnut shell to a sea shell or coconut shell. The container can be anything that can hold the cut plant materials. The old needlepoint, hairpin, shredded styrofoam, or chicken wire flower holders are still available and now the new and, in many ways more useful, floral foam materials have become a great step forward.

The standard annual and perennial garden flowers, along with their newly-bred cousins, offer a great opportunity for the modern-day flower arranger. Production of flowers in greenhouses and warmer outside areas in our southern states, plus foreign countries, have practically eliminated the seasonal shortages of the past. New and often exotic flowers are now avail-

Figure 4.2 A line-mass design of flowering branches, flowers, and greens with the candle as a focal point. (Courtesy Pennsylvania State University.)

able by air transport to meet the needs of the contemporary American floral market.

In summary, a knowledge of the history of flower arranging is important for the understanding of modern floral design. We have seen that today's American style of flower arranging has been influenced by the Oriental and European floral arts. It is characterized by clear-cut designs and forms, originality, and freedom of expression. In America, flower arrangements are used in many places in the home and provide a definite part of the decor.

part
II

THE
DESIGN

5

Design Styles in Flower Arranging

COMPOSITION AND DESIGN

Flower arrangers tend to use the words *composition* and *design* interchangeably, but this is technically incorrect. The *composition* refers to the final result, the achievement of the arranger. The flowers, plant materials, container, accessories, the background, and the setting in which the arrangement has been placed all combine to form a visual entity. You can stand back and view the composition.

The *design* is the concept, the plan. A design is a scheme for organizing and arranging components into a completed composition, into a work of art. A flower arranger creates a good floral composition by following principles of design, principles which are used in all the visual arts, including painting, sculpture, architecture, landscaping, and interior design.

In any style of flower arranging, past or present, American, European, or Oriental, there are six design elements to be considered. Five of these are line, form, space, texture, and color; line, form and space combine to form the sixth element: pattern.

There are also seven principles of design: balance, scale, harmony, rhythm, repetition, unity, and focus. The design elements will be discussed in detail in Chapters 6 and 7, and the design principles in Chapter 8. All the principles of design should be present in every good arrangement, but their relative importance will vary.

In any flower arrangement, there must be a definite relationship between the design elements—a feeling of security, naturalness, balance, and simplicity. In order to arrange flowers in such a manner, it is necessary to recognize all the elements of good design. There must be a basic idea, a mental picture, a conception of what you wish to create. Moreover, we need to consider where the arrangement is to be placed and the function it is to serve.

CONVENTIONAL STYLES OF FLOWER ARRANGING

American flower arrangements combine certain features of traditional European and Oriental arranging. The Japanese emphasis on line is combined with the dominance in European arrangements of masses of many kinds of plant materials and mixtures of color. American line-mass flower arrangements stress clear-cut designs, originality, and freedom of expression.

Three kinds of traditional flower arrangements are recognized today in America by flower arrangers and the National Council of State Garden Clubs.

Line arrangements are designed with visual paths along which the eye is led in a natural and logical sequence from one point of interest to another. The line or lines are usually so strong or obvious that they dominate the whole composition. In floral arrangements, these lines and identifiable points consist of blossoms, leaves, stems, or similar accents. The importance of each visual path is in direct proportion to its actual size, color value, and distinction of form. In line arrangements, the spaces and voids are often as important as the flower and plant materials.

Frequently, line arrangements are constructed entirely from lines and silhouettes of individual twigs, leaves, and/or flowers and it is the voids between them that form the design. This does not mean that line compositions are necessarily two-dimensional. The twigs, stems, and branches visually support each other in an overlapping fashion so that the eye is carried *into* the design as well as upward and to each side. Often the volume of the arrangement is too large, but the actual amount of plant material used is quite small. A typical line arrangement rarely uses massed materials to create a focal point; more often there is a convergence of the lines culminating in a single flower. It is difficult to create a line arrangement that can be used and seen from more than one side, so they are often called *one-sided* compositions. The balance in line arrangements is more often asymmetrical than symmetrical.

Mass arrangements are compositions in which the plant materials are of primary importance. Spaces and voids are present, but are smaller and less conspicuous than in line arrangements. The mass arrangement is frequently thought of as being physically large, but this need not be the case. Mass

Figure 5.1 An American design of bird-of-paradise flowers and foliage, with Ti leaves and asparagus. [See also Color Plate.] (Courtesy Teleflora, Inc.)

compositions tend to be more dense than line arrangements; although they may consist of only flowers or only foliages, most mass arrangements will contain both.

Arrangements may be designed for viewing from one side or from several angles, depending upon circumstances. Mass arrangements are often used as table centerpieces which are intended for viewing from all sides. Special attention is given to the dimension of depth in mass arrangements.

Line-mass arrangements (Figure 5.1), as the name suggests, are a combination of two styles. A definite line is visible in the materials used to create the arrangements, but more material is used than in a pure line arrangement. The arrangement is not as "full" or tightly packed as a traditional mass arrangement. It may be a very compact "small" mass with many kinds of plant materials and/or flowers as is frequently found in European arrangements.

The American style of flower arranging focuses primarily on arrangements of the line-mass style.

OTHER STYLES OF FLOWER ARRANGING

Creative people constantly seek new ways of expressing themselves, and flower arrangers are no exception. Therefore, we cannot arbitrarily classify all American arrangers as line-mass stylists. Some may prefer to identify their styles as naturalistic, free form, abstract, or some other type. The traditionalist may not accept or understand these designs, but the clash between the traditional and the avant-garde is typical of all art forms.

In the *naturalistic* style, the arranger portrays the natural growth pattern of the particular plant material being used. For example, the composition may consist of one or more stems of daylily or German iris, with the largest flower up high, emerging from a fan-shaped cluster of its own leaves.

The *free-form* stylist uses easily flowing lines and natural curves rather than straight lines, sharp angles, or precise curves. This preference precludes designs using geometric shapes such as the triangles, circles, crescents, right angles, and parabolas employed by traditional flower arrangers.

The *abstract* arranger combines plant materials with articles and materials not normally associated with plants to create compositions intended to break space into interesting patterns, or as a means to interpret or create a mood, idea, or theme. One type of such an arrangement is a collage in which flowers and other fragments and objects may be attached together and framed. Another is the assemblage which is a combination of flowers and other objects, anything from driftwood to machinery. Yet another type is the mobile or hanging sculpture.

This aspect of flower arranging is treated more fully in Chapter 22.

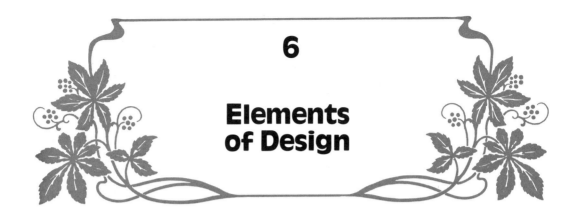

6

Elements of Design

Many people are attracted to flower arranging because of their love and respect for nature. Blossoms with their beautiful shapes, colors, textures, and perfumes; foliage in an infinite variety of shapes, patterns, and sizes; mosses, twigs, branches, fruits, and trees; the earth itself, its rocks, pebbles, and sands, are all aspects of nature that serve to intrigue and challenge us. The more experience we have arranging flowers, the more observant we become, discovering new worlds hidden in our everyday surroundings.

When flower arrangers create a composition, they take the materials they have selected and arrange them according to the elements and principles of design to attain beauty, expression, and harmony in the completed composition.

As we noted previously, the six elements of design are line, form, space, texture, color, and pattern. These are tangible physical characteristics that all objects possess. Each is distinct from the others, and each must be controlled by the designer to produce the desired overall result.

They are the ingredients or building blocks from which all flower arrangements, good and bad, are constructed.

LINE

Each piece of plant material used for making a flower arrangement possesses a visual lightness or heaviness related to line. A stem of *gladiolus* or snapdragon, a branch of a tree or shrub clearly represents a visual line. The line material may be straight or curved, short or long, thick or thin. It may have a stiff, spiky character, or a soft, pliable one. For our purposes, the terms *line* and *linear form* may be used interchangeably.

In every good design there is a skeleton or framework which is the underlying pattern that holds the whole composition together and gives it a foundation upon which to build. Line in flower arrangement is a visual path along which the eye is led, in a natural and logical sequence, from one point of interest to another. In flower arranging, these points consist of blossoms, leaves, stems, or any other accents.

Since lines create visual paths, they are useful in orienting the eye where we want it to move about in an arrangement. The path may be long or short, narrow or wide, angular, straight, or curved. If curved, it may curve swiftly or gently. It may close back on itself, either partially or completely, or it may reverse itself. It may be smooth and unbroken, or it may be interrupted by other lines so that its course is less dominant or bold. The path may be so bold and well-defined that the visual momentum will carry across a wide gap to pick up the course of another line. Visual paths, like foot paths, may be traveled in both directions.

Many arrangements start with a linear piece of plant material such as a narrow leaf, a twig, a branch, or a flower stalk. This linear piece must be placed firmly on the holder or other mechanical aid where it becomes the dominant line for the whole composition. From that point to the finished arrangement, everything used becomes subordinate in relation to the dominant line. It may curve ($\searc
row$), be vertical ($|$), horizontal (—), or diagonal ($/$), but there is always this line of emphasis that is the starting point. The horizontal line gives a feeling of tranquility and repose; the vertical line one of dignity, aspiration, and quiet movement upward; while the curve lends a feeling of movement to the arrangement.

The natural form of plant materials often serves as a guide for the selection of linear material. Branches or stems from the upper part of a plant or shrub are often suitable for vertical placement. Side branches are often more suitable for diagonal placement, while the lowest branches, since they have grown horizontally first, are often useful for low or horizontal placement. Plant material should be studied before it is cut to determine how effective a structural framework it can create. At the same time, the arranger must decide whether much of it must be trimmed to create a well-defined visual path.

Flowers with a linear form are not as common as those with a more rounded or weighty appearance. Many have only short blooming seasons, and others have only limited color variations. Linear flowers include snapdragons, stock, larkspur, *delphinium, plumed celosia, baptisia, gladiolus,* foxglove, loosestrife, *physostegia, salvia, buddleia, thermopsis, tritoma, veronica,* iris buds, calla buds, lupine, *penstemon,* and pencil statice.

When cut flowers are unavailable, the determined flower arranger will turn to other plant materials for linear accents. Special foliages such as spiral eucalyptus, *podocarpus*, fern fronds of many kinds (asparagus, Boston, ming, etc.), *sansevieria, gladiolus* leaves, are available much of the year from the garden or from the local florist shop. Many kinds of evergreen tree and shrub materials such as cedar, fir, pussy willows, scotch broom, *camellia,* are useful along with deciduous tree or vine boughs, with or without leaves, as raw linear material.

The first placement in a linear design must be bold and dominant. It gives character, force, and vigor to the arrangement. After that, imagination completes the picture with varying forms of plant materials, with contrast in textures, with foliage and blossoms and color, and perhaps with unexpected "found objects" from anywhere.

Line is much less dominant in a mass arrangement, although the majority of American flower arrangements are line-mass compositions, as we have mentioned.

FORM

Form, in flower arrangement, is the general outline created by the plant materials. It is the outward contour of all individual components, as well as the whole design. A person viewing a flower arrangement should be able to recognize some familiar geometric form. Flower arrangers must always remember that they are working in all three dimensions—height, width, and depth (Figure 6.1).

The three-dimensional geometric forms which are basic to good flower arranging are the pyramid, the cone, the sphere, the cube, and the cylinder,

Figure 6.1 Placement of flowers to give the third dimension (depth) in flower arranging. (Courtesy Washington State University.)

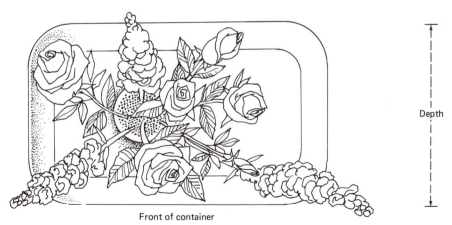

Front of container

Depth

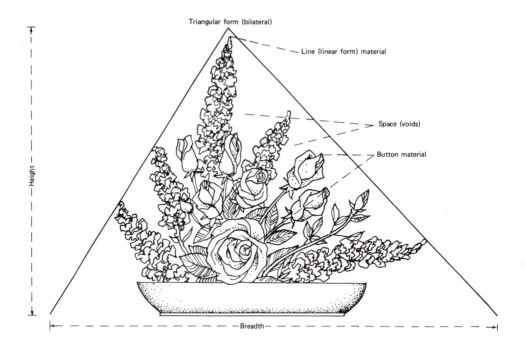

Figure 6.2 Triangular form as a design element in flower arranging. (Courtesy Washington State University.)

or portions of these shapes. We often work with two-dimensional diagrams and sketches, but we must always remain conscious of the three-dimensional form of the arrangement (Figure 6.2).

In the American style of flower arranging, there are four basic forms: (1) horizontal, (2) vertical, (3) triangular, and (4) radial. The horizontal and vertical forms are monolinear (one-line) designs, while the triangular and radial are bilinear (two-line) designs. All acceptable flower arrangements use one of the four forms, or a modification or combination of them (Figure 6.3).

American flower arrangements are considered to follow one of thirteen design forms: horizontal, S-curve or Hogarth curve, vertical, inverted-T, symmetrical triangle, asymmetrical triangle, right angle, crescent, circle, oval, zigzag, spiral, or diagonal (Figure 6.4).

Shapes related to a pyramid or cone produce a feeling of stability in an arrangement; shapes akin to a sphere or oval, serenity. The vertical or horizontal accents give a feeling of pleasure because of the long dominant lines; the fanning out of a pyramid gives a festive feeling; and the S-curve a feeling of grace and charm.

Horizontal lines are popular for use in table centerpieces and arrangements on coffee tables, mantles, or wherever the background demands a long, low arrangement. They are useful for church altars and have a restfu effect. Spike flowers emphasize the horizontal effect and round flowers create the focal point as well as filling in around the spikes (Figure 6.5).

Vertical lines are the most natural to use because most flowers and plants grow vertically. These lines suggest growth and vigor. The vertical arrangement fits in very well in the contemporary American home where it can be framed by a particular spot in the room (Figures 6.6 and 6.7).

Although the spiral is often thought of as a "figure 9," a modern adaptation of this form appears in Figure 6.8, which shows dried blackboy grass coming through 'Princess Michiko' roses and twirling around the pods of Kipoh creeper. This device gives an excellent feeling of motion to the arrangement.

The triangle is said to be the most popular compositional form in all pictorial art. It is one of the most pleasing and probably the easiest form to use in flower arranging. The flower arranger may use the pyramid or symmetrical triangle (Figure 6.9), the asymmetrical triangle, the right-angled or L-shaped triangle (Figure 6.10), or the open triangle. All these forms have depth or a third dimension in the flower arrangement. The two newest forms in flower arranging are the right-angle triangle and the open triangle. Both employ voids in their design. These designs are economical because they use fewer flowers and are especially adapted to the modern home. A variation of the open triangle is the inverted-T, or the inverted-Y.

Radial lines in flower arrangements form part of a circle, which holds the motion of the eye within the design. The focal point acts like the hub of a wheel (Figures 6.11 and 6.12). Motion is also exemplified in the S or Hogarth curve.

SPACE

In floral design we are dealing with defined space, with real or specified boundaries. There are three kinds of space for us to consider: the space which encompasses the whole floral arrangement, the spaces inherent within the plant and other materials used in the arrangement, and the spaces created within the arrangement.

The total space is defined by the background and its frame. When the background is intimate or close, it creates a frame that is fixed and predetermined. When the background is distant or changeable, and yet provides a visual frame, the space available in which to arrange is more variable but it too has some limitations: the perspective of the viewer, the size and shape of the arrangement's resting place, the height from the floor, the viewing angle and the distance from which the arrangement is viewed may limit the composition.

Each piece of plant material used in a flower arrangement has an inher-

Horizontal

Hogarth

Vertical

Inverted 'T'

Right-Angle

Asymmetrical Triangle

Symmetrical Triangle

Figure 6.3 The 13 basic geometric forms for floral design. (Courtesy Pennsylvania State University.)

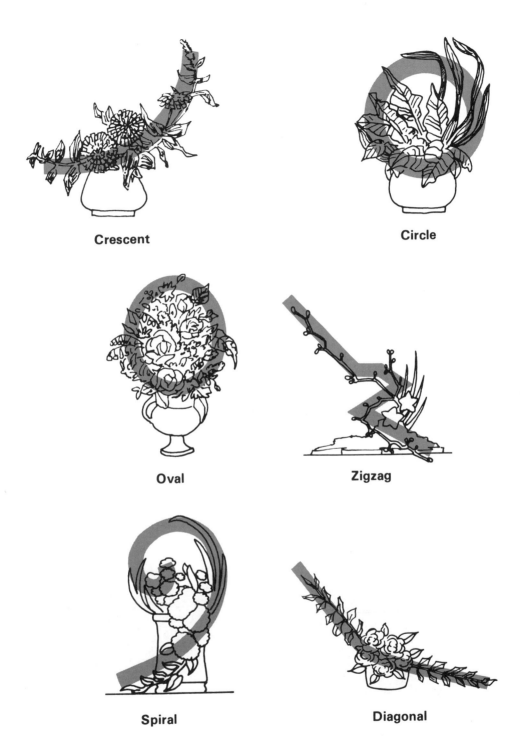

Crescent

Circle

Oval

Zigzag

Spiral

Diagonal

Figure 6.3 (continued)

Symmetrical Triangle

The full or *symmetrical* triangle with all sides equal is a popular form with the beginner. By shortening the base line and keeping side lines the same length, a more slender length triangle is produced.

The *asymmetrical* triangle is similar to a scalene triangle with one side much longer than the other. It is one of the most favored designs for flower arrangers and has many uses.

Asymmetrical Triangle

Right-Angle

The *right-angle* triangle is an L-shaped arrangement similar to an asymmetrical triangle but using a void instead of being filled in solid. It uses fewer flowers and is a more modern type of design than some of the others.

Figure 6.4 Descriptions of the 13 basic geometric forms. (Courtesy Pennsylvania State University.)

Heavier and larger flowers in the center of the design give a feeling of stability to the *horizontal* form. Horizontal lines extend over the sides of the container. While tips of lines are low, they should not touch the table.

Horizontal

The *Hogarth* line, which suggests a slender S with slow graceful curves, gives a feeling of rhythm. It is well adapted to upright arrangements, but may also be used in a horizontal position. It is very versatile in that the artist may make an arrangement in a slight or deep 'S', a backward 'S', or a low horizontal 'S'. The Hogarth curve was named after the English painter and engraver (1697–1764) who signed his work with a serpentine curve called 'the line of beauty'.

Hogarth

Tall, slender lines used in the *vertical* form carry the eye upward and give a feeling of dignity. Such an arrangement is effective in a narrow space such as between windows or against tall, narrow panels.

Vertical

The *inverted T,* or *open* triangle, is a modern concept of the regular symmetrical triangle plus the Japanese influence. It employs the use of voids in the design and uses fewer flowers than the conventional triangle. An adaptation of the open triangle is the inverted Y, in which the two width flowers go out to the front at an angle rather than in a straight line as is seen in the inverted T.

Inverted 'T'

Figure 6.4 (continued)

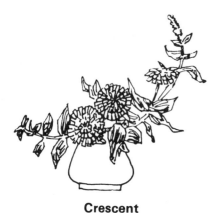

Crescent

Skill is required to give a feeling of balance to the *crescent* form. Use flower stems that can be curved gracefully. Tips of a crescent may be brought closer together. It is asymmetrical in design.

In this *circle* a feeling of motion is created with graceful curving lines that almost meet. Heavier flowers and broader leaves are used low in the arrangement to break the line of the container.

Circle

The *oval* form suggests mass arrangement. By keeping the smaller, lighter-colored flowers on outer edges and the larger, stronger-colored ones at low center of oval, a fine sense of balance is achieved.

Oval

Figure 6.4 (continued)

The *zigzag* is used when the arranger has picked some very unusual twiggy material such as hawthorne branches that give a zigzag effect. Balance is the hardest part in achieving a pleasing effect in this design.

Zigzag

The *spiral* is a design shaped like a figure 9. It consists of a crescent with a tail on it and is only used for fun when trying something different. The other types of design are usually preferred. A more pleasing adaptation of the spiral is found in using flowers around a candle in a real spiral effect much as is found in a spiral staircase around a center pole.

Spiral

The *diagonal* design must not be an absolutely straight line. It has a slight dog-leg effect and is most pleasing in a pedestal container. It is in between a vertical and a right-angle triangle.

Diagonal

Figure 6.4 (continued)

Figure 6.5 A horizontal arrangement of callas by E. W. Kalin. (Courtesy WSU Photo, Washington State University.)

Figure 6.6 A vertical arrangement of snapdragons and carnations by E. W. Kalin. (Courtesy WSU Photo, Washington State University.)

An American design of bird-of-paradise flowers and foliage, with Ti leaves and asparagus.
(Courtesy Teleflora, Inc.)

A vertical arrangement of carnations in a tall, cylindrical container.
(Courtesy FTDA.)

A typical American symmetrical flower arrangement. (**Courtesy FTDA.**)

Red *gladioli* and *draceana* foliage contrast beautifully in a white container. (**Courtesy Teleflora, Inc.**)

A collection of dried materials in a vertical arrangement. (**Courtesy Teleflora, Inc.**)

A lovely table centerpiece with candles and place settings as accessories. (**Courtesy Teleflora, Inc.**)

Fantastique. (Courtesy Mrs. H.E. Brown, Ozona, FL.)

Four *cymbidiums* for a fine Mother's Day arrangement. (Courtesy FTDA.)

A mixed basket of flowers. (Courtesy FTDA.)

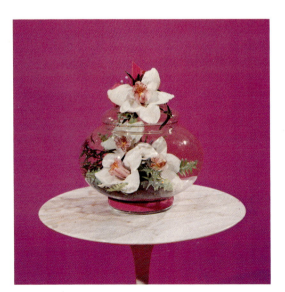

Figure 6.7 A vertical arrangement of carnations in a tall, cylindrical container. [See also Color Plate.] (Courtesy FTDA.)

Figure 6.8 *Blast Off,* an example of a modern spiral arrangement. (Courtesy Mrs. E. R. Cottrill, Melbourne, Australia.)

Figure 6.9 A fine symmetrical triangle of daffodils. (Courtesy Teleflora, Inc.)

Figure 6.10 Simplicity shows up attractively in an L-shaped (right-angle) triangle of greens and orchids. (Courtesy Teleflora, Inc.)

Figure 6.11 A fine example of the Hogarth (S) curve. (Courtesy Teleflora, Inc.)

Figure 6.12 A radial arrangement of *gladioli* and roses by E. W. Kalin. (Courtesy WSU Photo, Washington State University.)

ent spatial characteristic. Individual petals, flowers, or foliages create unique spaces. Take, for example, an iris: the standards (upright portion) loosely enclose space and the falls (pendulous portion) suggest broken space.

The two kinds of space discussed above—the background and its visual frame and the spatial characteristic—are ones over which the flower arranger has only limited control; however, the space involved within the arrangement is under the complete control of the artist. The moment a flower arranger picks up a vase or a bowl to begin work, he has already made a fundamental choice about space. Flower arranging at its heart consists of "breaking up" space into interesting patterns. The empty portions of the arrangement are the spaces of interest within the design. These empty spaces are just as important as are the plant materials. In a line arrangement the spaces or voids may be approximately equal in size to the plant material, while in the mass arrangement the volume of plant materials exceeds the volume of empty space. The American line-mass arrangement is a compromise between the two. Space is a definite part of the complete composition which ties in with the external silhouette of the arrangement. The spaces between the forms and lines of the arrangement should have interesting variations. The voids are most frequently open toward the outer areas of the composition.

PATTERN

Pattern is a combination of lines, forms, and the spaces between them. It is present in plant material as well as in the ultimate design. Pattern is the silhouette of the arrangement against the background. It is the element of design which may involve the wall with a piece of tapestry forming the background for the floral design. It also refers to the image on the table upon which the arrangement may be placed. This forms a pattern which is included in the composition. Often the pattern will form a silhouette against a plain wall in the home to give a very pleasing and sometimes startling effect.

TEXTURE

Texture is the quality of the surface of a material, what it looks like and what it feels like. Everything we see and touch has a texture—rough or smooth, coarse or fine, glossy or dull, hard or soft.

There is no sharp line between form and texture. When forms become so small that the viewer does not experience them individually, they become texture. For example, a hydrangea flower is considered a coarse flower. In reality, the coarse "flower" is a series of many small florets whose petals are spaced at sharp angles to each other and are not at all coarse in texture. Flower forms that appear as individual parts of an arrangement may appear as texture in a photograph of the arrangement. Foliage that has individual form in an arrangement becomes texture when it becomes part of the landscape. The proximity and angle from which a flower arrangement and its various plant materials are viewed affects the textural qualities of the materials.

The arranger must consider the texture not only of the flowers, foliages, and plant materials, but also of the container and those objects in the immediate area where the arrangement is to be placed. Most flower arrangers catalogue in their minds the flowers and foliages that are, for example, fine-textured: hybrid tea roses, orchids, pompon chrysanthemums, asparagus fern, and so forth. An experienced flower arranger normally would not use roses and orchids in Mexican pottery any more than you would use marigolds and zinnias in your best crystal or silver—each would look quite out of place. But when the combinations are reversed, we realize the marigolds would be perfect in Mexican pottery as would roses in a silver bowl. Textures of flowers and foliages should be reasonably related to each other in order to blend together into a harmonious arrangement.

The extremes of texture—coarse or fine, smooth or rough, bright or dull, and so on—are strongest. "In-between" textures are weaker. The texture of shiny unbroken surfaces is strong because of the amount of light reflected from them. Rough textures are strong because the sharp contrast of light and dark areas defines these areas so that many small forms are recognizable. So the very smooth texture of glazed ceramic and the very coarse texture of, say, tree bark, are stronger than the in-between textures of most foliage. Smooth textures attract attention quickly, but rough textures tend to hold attention longer; it takes the eye longer to wander over rough texture, to encompass all the value it offers.

The in-between textures of many kinds of foliage are among the most important tools available to the flower arranger. The inherent elements in foliage are intermediate forms, static colors, and in-between textures. The in-betweens are passive and restful. They are the harmonizers in contrived and natural landscapes, and serve the same purpose in floral design.

Texture is also related to color and can modify color value. Since color is reflected light, the physical structure (texture) of the reflecting surface affects color. The smooth unbroken surface will reflect colors with full intensity, while rough surfaces will not.

Flower containers, an important aspect of good flower design, have various textures, depending upon their material and finish. The designer must relate the texture of the container to the textures of the plant materials. The American style of flower arranging uses a wide variety of containers, from classic alabaster and crystal to a hollowed-out pumpkin or coconut. The texture of the container should be compatible in appearance and association with the plant materials to produce a completely related composition.

Besides the textures of flowers, foliages, and containers, the arranger should also consider the texture of the surroundings, which must blend with the arrangement to produce a harmonious effect. Sometimes a contrast in the textures, or a variety of textures, may be the best way to achieve an effective and distinctive design. There are many textures from which to choose for designing each part of the flower arrangement.

7

Color Concerns in Flower Arranging

SELECTION AND USE OF COLORS IN FLOWER ARRANGEMENTS

Since color provides the most striking visual effect of flowers, it plays an important part in each arrangement. A color is affected by light, background, neighboring colors, surface texture, flower form, and distance. Color brings life to flower arrangements, as it does to rooms or clothes, just as the melody brings life to music.

Knowledge of color and color harmonies is essential for good flower arranging. All colors are beautiful, but a poor color combination can produce an unpleasant effect. Each person "sees" color a little differently because of personality and experience. People also literally see color differently because eyes have different sensitivities.

Color affects people emotionally. Everyone reacts to the beauty of a sunset. Color sets the tone of a flower arrangement, which may be cheerful, drab, formal or informal, naturalistic, sturdy, delicate, or bizarre. Flowers are translucent while pigments are opaque, so we have two different color media with which to work. The true blue of a flower may not match the true blue of a vase. The texture, pigment quality, and hue make the difference.

Color is a general term, and we often use it when we mean *hue*.

COLOR TERMINOLOGY

Color has a language of its own. The following terms are used to describe color quality:

1. *Hue* is the colors of the spectrum; the name of color; the quality or difference between one color and another, as red and yellow. Value depends upon the amount of white or black that is mixed with a hue. If white is added to red, the result is pink. Pink is a light value of red.

2. *Tint* is a hue plus white. Tints are lighter than hues of the spectrum.

3. *Shade* is a hue plus black. Shades are darker than hues of the spectrum.

4. *Intensity (chroma)* is the degree of intensity or purity of a hue. When a hue is mixed with gray *(tone)* or with a small amount of a hue from the opposite side of the color wheel, it becomes less intense. Pure yellow is clear and bright. Adding gray or a small amount of violet makes it softer and less intense.

EMOTIONAL RESPONSE TO COLOR

Various colors will produce different emotional and psychological effects. Certain colors seem warm or cool because they are associated with objects that are warm or cool. Red and yellow seem to give a warm feeling because they are the colors of fire and sunlight. Blue and green seem cool because they are the colors of sky, water, ice, and foliage. The *color wheel* (see Figures 7.1 and 7.2 and the inside front and back covers) may be divided roughly in half with the warm colors on one side and the cool colors on the other side. Thus, blue-green through violet-blue to violet-red give us a cool feeling, while red through yellow-orange to yellow-green have a warm effect. Green and red may be either warm or cool, depending upon whether there is more yellow (warm) or more blue (cool) in the red or green shades.

To achieve a feeling of cheerfulness, brightness, and warmth in a flower arrangement, use yellow, orange, or red in various tints and tones, or use a combination of them. Blue and blue-greens are cool and refreshing. Violets and purples give a spiritual feeling, sometimes sad, while black and dark shades may produce a depressing effect. Tints of various hues will normally be uplifting, while tones tend to give a soothing effect. White can be either warm or cool, it takes on the feelings of the colors with which it is associated. White unites discordant hues. Green, because of its natural

the basics of Color

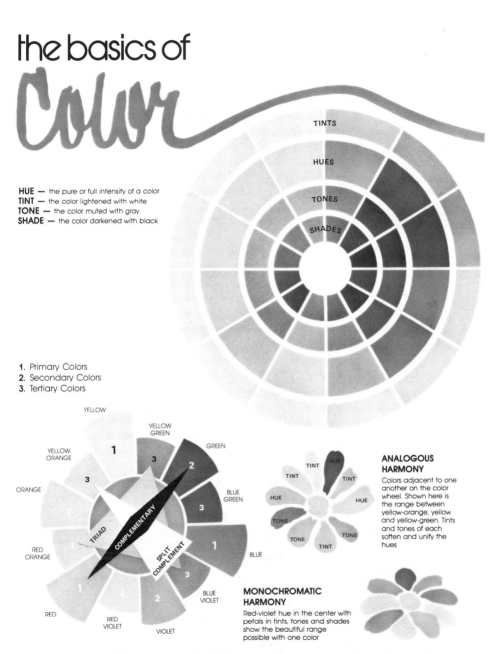

HUE — the pure or full intensity of a color
TINT — the color lightened with white
TONE — the color muted with gray
SHADE — the color darkened with black

TINTS
HUES
TONES
SHADES

1. Primary Colors
2. Secondary Colors
3. Tertiary Colors

YELLOW
YELLOW GREEN
GREEN
YELLOW ORANGE
ORANGE
BLUE GREEN
RED ORANGE
BLUE
RED
BLUE VIOLET
RED VIOLET
VIOLET

TRIAD
COMPLEMENTARY
SPLIT COMPLEMENT

ANALOGOUS HARMONY
Colors adjacent to one another on the color wheel. Shown here is the range between yellow-orange, yellow and yellow-green. Tints and tones of each soften and unify the hues

TINT HUE TINT
HUE HUE
TONE TONE
TONE TINT

MONOCHROMATIC HARMONY
Red-violet hue in the center with petals in tints, tones and shades show the beautiful range possible with one color

Figure 7.1 A 12-hue color wheel. [See also inside front cover.] (Courtesy Teleflora, Inc.)

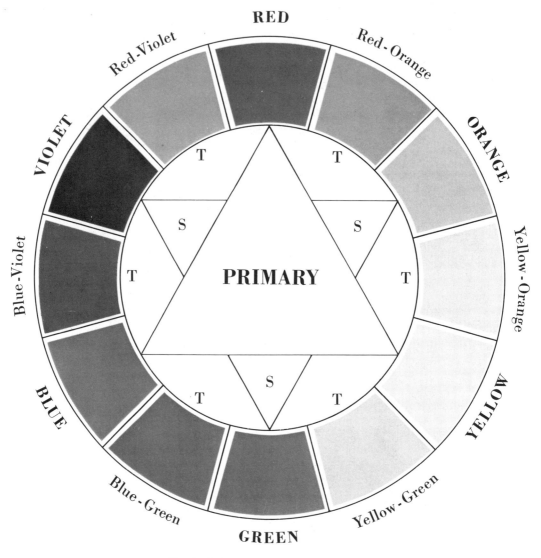

The color wheel shows an orderly arrangement of the basic colors—primary, secondary, and tertiary—and is helpful in selecting and mixing. The use of color in rendering, as well as the specifying of colors for other architectural applications, must start with a familiarity of the color wheel if pleasing combinations are to be achieved. (See Sec. 13.6, p. 365.)

Figure 7.2 Primary, secondary, and tertiary colors on the color wheel. [See also inside back cover.] (Source: E. Muller, *Architectural Drawing and Light Construction,* 2/E, © 1976, front inside cover. Reprinted by permission of Prentice-Hall, Inc.)

Figure 7.3 A typical American symmetrical flower arrangement. [See also Color Plate.](Courtesy FTDA.)

occurrence in plant materials, has a unifying effect within an arrangement. (See color photos, pages 53 to 56.)

COLOR VISIBILITY AND INTENSITY

Warm colors have high visibility and seem to advance toward the viewer, while cool colors have low visibility and tend to appear to recede. Intense colors advance more than those tones in which gray has been mixed with the pure hue. Yellow has the highest visibility, violet the lowest. These factors enter into and determine the function that various hues will serve in a flower arrangement.

Black is the absence of all colors; white, the presence of all colors. Black, white, and gray are all neutral colors which we use in flower arranging in combination with hues. The blacks and grays are found in the accessories and background items used in and around the completed composition, since we rarely find flowers that are truly black or gray.

Color is relative because one color is used in combination with others. This may change the apparent hue. The color of the background may change the effect of the whole flower arrangement. Different kinds of lighting may change the color. Blues and violets are often lost under artificial lights, for example, and red roses and red poinsettias lose much of their appeal under cool white fluorescent lights (Figures 7.4 and 7.5).

Figure 7.4 White carnations and pink roses blend perfectly in a low, white bowl. (Courtesy Pennsylvania State University.)

Figure 7.5 Red *gladioli* and *dracaena* foliage contrast beautifully in a white container. [See also Color Plate.] (Courtesy Teleflora, Inc.)

The flower show exhibitor may have a brilliant arrangement at home, but when the ensemble is brought to the show it may be much less spectacular because of a limited amount of light in the exhibition area.

The color coordination chart shown in Table 7-1 shows the importance of the various backgrounds to flowers of the six principal colors in the spectrum.

Since the quality of balance in a flower arrangement is usually the visual balance (see Chapter 8) perceived by the eye of the designer, the ways that colors and their uses affect this balance is particularly important to the design of flower arrangements. Flowers of dark colors such as red, maroon, dark purple, or dark blue are visually heavier than the lighter, warmer colors of yellow, pink, orange, or yellow-greens, even though they may be the same size physically. Because the dark colors have more visual weight they are usually placed low in the design to give stability.

In order to achieve good color balance when two or three colors are used in a single flower arrangement, it helps to avoid using them in equal volume.

Color intensity may be used to create the center of interest and/or the focal point of the composition, although the focal point is more frequently obtained by using a flower, or a group of flowers, that is visually and physically larger.

Light intensity plays an important role in evaluating a flower arrangement. No object can reflect more light than is directed on it, and since color is only reflected light, it is natural that the brighter the light, the stronger the color, and the weaker the light, the weaker the colors.

Table 7-1 *A color coordinating chart*

Color of merchandise	Black background	White background	Light background	Dark gray background
Yellow	richness enhanced	slightly duller	warmer	brighter
Red	far more brilliant	darker, purer	bright, but less intense	brighter, but loses saturation
Blue	more luminous	richer and darker	a little more luminous	brighter
Green	paler, sharpened	deepens in value	takes on yellowish cast	brightens, gray becomes reddish
Orange	more luminous	darker and redder	lighter and yellowish	increases brilliancy
Purple	loses strength and brilliancy	darker	brighter, gray becomes greenish	gray becomes green

SOURCE: Kenneth H. Mill and Judith E. Paul, *Create Distinctive Display*, © 1974, p. 86. Reprinted by permission of Prentice-Hall, Inc.

PIGMENT THEORY COLOR WHEEL

There are several theories of color used in art, physics, chemistry, and psychology. Each employs a different color theory because it is concerned with different aspects of the study of color.

The pigment theory of color is the most practical for flower arranging and is the one that we will discuss in some detail. The pigment theory shows us how all colors are related. This knowledge, together with the vocabulary of color as developed within the pigment theory, serves as a valuable tool in the study of color. The spectrum is a progression of hues: red, orange, yellow, green, blue, and violet. The hues are always in the same order with red having the longest wave length and violet the shortest. When these hues are placed in a circle in order a *color wheel* is formed by which we clarify our understanding of color harmony.

The *primary* colors in the pigment system are red, yellow, and blue, so called because they cannot be made by mixing any of the colors together. By the same token, all other colors are made by mixing these three colors in varying amounts.

The *secondary* colors are orange, green, and violet. They are obtained by mixing equal amounts of two adjacent primary colors: orange from yellow and red; green from yellow and blue; and violet from red and blue. The three primary colors along with the three secondary colors are usually called the six standard colors.

Tertiary or *intermediate* colors come from combining a primary color with a secondary color. The tertiary colors are red-orange, yellow-orange, yellow-green, blue-green, blue-violet, and red-violet. Although a color wheel may show six, twelve, or eighteen colors, the twelve-color wheel is the one most often used by teachers of flower arranging.

COLOR HARMONY

Combining certain primary, secondary, and tertiary colors can produce color harmony. The successful arranger learns to combine colors which are harmonious. Most people have an intuitive sense of color combinations and harmonies, but skill in color selection is something that can be sharpened and broadened with study and experience.

Related Harmonies

Monochromatic Color Harmony. Monochromatic color harmony is achieved by using tints, tones, and shades of one hue. This one-hued harmony is made up of several values and intensities of hues. An example is the combination of tints, tones, and shades of browns in an autumnal arrangement of dried plants. The container might well be brown to harmonize with the colors of the plant materials. Another example is an all-green arrangement of foliages. Monochromatic harmony can run the whole scale of one hue from light to dark and from bright to dull. This is probably the easiest scheme for a beginner. Monochromatic arrangements are particularly appropriate in rooms which already have great variety in the color and pattern of their interior design.

Analogous Color Harmony. Analogous or neighboring color harmony uses two or three adjacent colors on the color wheel. This harmony is one primary color with one or two secondary or tertiary colors. Use no more than one primary color. The values and intensities of the different hues may be varied. An example would be orange, yellow-orange, and yellow used together. One color should dominate in order to unify the total effect. The various tints, tones, and shades of adjacent hues may also be used in analogous color harmony. They should be either all warm or all cool colors.

Contrasting Harmonies

The remaining four color harmonies are nonrelated or contrasting. They are made up of various combinations of colors that are opposite or nearly opposite to each other on the color wheel.

Direct Complement. A direct complement is one of the most stimulating and most often used techniques in flower arranging. Two colors directly opposite each other on the wheel are chosen. Examples would be red and green, violet and yellow, or red-orange with green-blue. This type of combination gives the greatest contrast, but to be successful the two hues must be used in unequal amounts. We avoid choosing equal quantitites of the same value or intensity; we would have some light colors, some medium, or some dark, some bright, some dull. When warm and cool colors are combined, this scheme offers greater contrast than any other color harmony. It is one of the most popular harmonies used in flower arranging today. Direct complementary colors—colors exactly opposite each other on the color wheel—enhance each other's brilliance. They express boldness. Red and green for Christmas is a favorite direct complementary schedule typified in nature by the red poinsettia with its green foliage.

Split Complement. A split complement consists of one color plus the two colors on either side of the direct complement. The colors which stand on either side of the direct complement balance the complement; thus, blue-green and yellow-green balance red; or orange-yellow and green-yellow balance violet. It is a harmony of three colors only. Again, the best results occur with one color dominating, with some intensities reduced, and with a variation in the values.

Triad. A triad is composed of any three colors which are equidistant on the color wheel. Thus, the primary colors of red, yellow, and blue comprise a triad. So do the secondary colors of orange, green, and violet; the tertiary colors of yellow-green, blue-violet, and red-orange are other examples. Any tints, tones, and/or shades of these three colors may be used. Again, one color should dominate.

Tetrad. The tetrad or paired complement is a harmony of four colors which are equidistant on the color wheel. Or, to state it another way, it is two pairs of direct complements at right angles to each other. The tetrad is not used as often as the other harmonies in flower arranging because it is generally best to use one, two, or three colors only.

POLYCHROMATIC HARMONIES (WILLIAMSBURG)

In recent years, many flower arrangers have become interested in making flower arrangements similar to those popular during the colonial period of America. Mrs. Louise B. Fisher, who was in charge for many years of all the flower arrangements made in restored Colonial Williamsburg, Virginia, wrote and published a book, and also made a film of the same title, *Flower Arrangements of Williamsburg.* The book and film are given much credit for stimulating this interest. Many of the arrangements by Mrs. Fisher and her assistant Betsy Meyers were made with many different tints, shades, and tones of a variety of hues. These are difficult and demanding arrangements to reproduce.

OTHER COLOR THEORIES

In physics, the three primary colors are considered to be red, green, and blue. Physicists view the visible spectrum as merely a segment of the electromagnetic spectrum. The psychological theory of color, on the other hand, is based on the visual perception of light, with red, green, yellow, and blue being the primary colors. Orange, yellow-green, blue-green, and violet are the secondary colors.

The Munsell system is based on a color circle of five principal hues and five intermediate hues. The principal hues are red, yellow, green, blue, and purple; the five intermediate colors are yellow-red, green-yellow, blue-green, purple-blue, and red-purple. This system is used to precisely describe the hue, value, and intensity of any color by means of values represented on a vertical scale on which zero is black, ten is white, with nine degrees of gray in between. Intensity (chroma) is represented on a horizontal scale with zero as gray and extending to varying degrees of intensity. It is interesting to note that the complementary color to red in the Munsell system is blue-green whereas in the pigment system it is green. Also, the intensity of the ten hues is not always in the middle of the value scale. Yellow achieves its greatest intensity at a higher value, or nearer white, and blue-purple at a lower value, or nearer black, than the other hues.

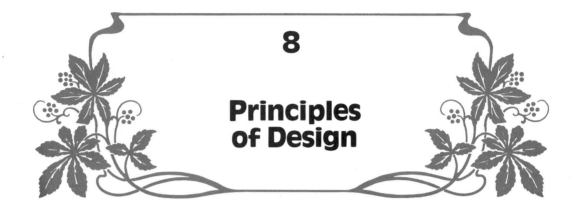

8

Principles of Design

The American style of flower arranging is based on the six elements of design already discussed: line, form, space, pattern, texture, and color, together with the seven principles of design to be covered in this chapter. These principles need to be combined with the six elements of design to achieve a successful flower arrangement.

The principles of design presented in this chapter are balance, scale, harmony, rhythm, repetition, unity, and focus or accent.

✗ BALANCE

and
Focus
is
Import.

Balance creates an impression of stability. The arrangement should not appear ready to fall over. Balance in a flower arrangement involves both physical and visual weight. The visual weight of each piece of plant material is determined by its color, distance from the established axis or focal point, and tonal value or lightness and darkness. Physical weight, the relative heaviness of materials being used together and the gradation of plant materials from the top of the arrangement to the base or bottom, is also important. The lightest and smallest flowers should be placed at the outer extremities of the arrangement and heaviest and largest flowers at the center, base, or bottom of the composition. In order to avoid a precarious balance, it is desirable that the tallest part of the flower arrangement not be too far away from the actual center of the container being used.

To avoid an arrangement that looks top-heavy, draw an imaginary horizontal line halfway up the arrangement and make sure there is more plant material below the line than above it.

Two kinds of balance are used in all the arts: symmetrical and asymmetrical.

Symmetrical Balance. With a symmetrical, conventional, or formal balance, an imaginary line can be drawn through the center of the arrangement which would divide it visually into two equal parts. Symmetrical balance is often found in arrangements based upon vertical, horizontal, and radial designs (see Chapter 6). The two sides need not be absolutely identical, but to be symmetrical should appear approximately the same—things are never identical in nature (Figure 8.1).

Figure 8.1 An arrangement that is symmetrically balanced. (Courtesy Teleflora, Inc.)

Asymmetrical Balance. Asymmetrical, or naturalistic or informal balance is the counterbalancing of unequal parts. The sides of the centerline are different in design but equal in *visual* weight. Asymmetrical balance operates on the principle of a seesaw: a large, heavy person must move quite close to the center to balance a small person on the far end of the board. Thus, large, dark flowers may be placed low and near the center of an arrangement while smaller, lighter flowers are placed at the edges.

Flowers may be bunched together and used as a unit to give them more visual weight. The asymmetrical or naturalistic form of balance permits more variation in placing the plant material in the floral arrangement (Figure 8.2).

Figure 8.2 An asymmetrical triangle of snapdragons and iris. (Courtesy Pennsylvania State University.)

SCALE

Scale is the actual and apparent size relationship of the components of an arrangement. The size of the flowers, foliage, container, and background should be reasonably related to each other. Because the visual measure or value of scale involves the relationship of many elements in a flower arrangement, and also its intended use, it is one of the most difficult principles of design to recognize, learn, or teach.

Make sure that the sizes of all the various components in an arrangement are consistently related. For example, large chrysanthemums with miniature roses would be out of scale, as would large calla leaves with small violet foliage. A large rose (four inches in diameter) in a miniature (two-inch) container would certainly be out of scale; the effect would be overpowering and topheavy.

A reasonable guide for the flower arranger is: flowers and foliage in an arrangement should be one and a half times as high as the average width of a low container or bowl and one and a half to two times as high as the height of an upright container or vase. When very light, airy, or fragile materials (flowering shrub or tree material, frail vines, grass plumes, delicate evergreen, spiral baby eucalyptus, etc.) are used, the flower arrangement may be two and a half to three times as tall as the upright container.

Scale is particularly important in miniature arrangements. If accessories such as a figurine are used in a composition, they should be in scale. Most plant material is "life-size," while figurines are usually scaled down. The human figure may be reduced to various sizes; an elephant may be reduced considerably; a butterfly or bird may be reduced only a little. This is also true for inanimate objects such as wishing wells, fans, crosses, etc., which may be variously reduced. Make these objects visually scaled to the overall situation.

Scale is also important when considering the background, such as a niche for an arrangement, or the size of the table for a table arrangement.

The container itself must be of the appropriate size to be in scale with the flowers, foliage, and setting. However, a definite flower-to-container-size ratio would be impossibly restrictive.

HARMONY

Proper harmony creates a satisfying relationship between all the materials used in a flower arrangement, along with the container, the setting, and its use. Many people are sensitive to a lack of color harmony; but harmony in flower arranging also involves texture, shape, size, and design. When all parts of the composition are in harmony, the result is an aesthetic whole. Aesthetic quality, of course, entails personal, emotional judgment.

The container should harmonize with the flowers and plant materials in its design, weight, and feeling. Using large, coarse flowers such as giant zinnias in a delicate crystal container creates poor harmony. The flowers and foliage should have something in common with each other in size, shape, texture, idea, time of flowering, and color. A combination of spring-flowering hyacinths and summer-flowering *delphiniums*, for instance, is usually incongruous and therefore is not harmonious either in size or seasonal relationship. A combination of asters and orchids may blend well in color but they are completely unrelated in texture and aesthetic qualities.

The texture of the flowers and the foliages selected must blend together in a pleasing fashion. The foliage which naturally comes with the flowers has a "built-in" relationship but it may be unsuitable with another flower or a different unrelated foliage. Calla leaves and roses are not a recommended combination. Carnation foliage and blue spruce are a complementary combination because each has an agreeable texture and a similar blue-green color. The foliage of a particular flower will be harmonious with that flower and should be used unless it has an offensive odor, or does not hold up well. We would not use daffodil foliages with carnations unless there were some daffodils in the arrangement. A coarse foliage such as that of salal would not harmonize effectively with roses or carnations, but could be used with *gladiolus*.

RHYTHM

Rhythm is achieved by relating the component parts of the flower arrangement so that the viewer's eye is guided through the design with a feeling of "swing" or motion. It requires an easily connected visual path along which the eye travels through the arrangement following lines, forms, gradations of colors, and contrasting light and dark areas.

Rhythmic motion in a flower arrangement is developed in various ways. Rhythm may be created by the repetition of color, shape, form, or line. The method for achieving the desirable, yet elusive, quality of rhythm is through the systematic and proper way of placing the various flowers and foliages. The repetition of flower forms and colors, the progression in spacing between flowers, and the subtle repetition of curves and planes all make their contribution to creating a rhythmic effect. If a particular flower appears in an arrangement, the eye should move rhythmically from one similar flower to another instead of continuously encountering something new.

Rhythm implies repetition but it must not lead to dullness. To avoid monotony, strive for more than one type of flower form. The ideal combination is to use a combination of spike and round flowers. The spike flowers because of their inherent linear form suggest a visual line. The round flowers are useful for emphasis. However, the proper placement of round flowers can create the illusion of line. In the absence of spike flowers, the round flowers can be placed in the top and edge portions of the arrangement in a loose line configuration with a strong profile view. We then gradually place them at an increasing angle as they descend in the arrangement toward the base where they show themselves full face (Figure 8.3).

Visual motion may also be created by varying the spacing between flowers from top to bottom, side to side, and front to back in the arrangement. Areas between flowers at the top and edges should be the largest, and they should decrease toward the base and from the edges to the center of the arrangement. The same sort of progression also applies to color, with light flowers toward the top and edges shifting to darker flowers at the base and center. Flower sizes should follow a similar pattern: physically and visually smaller flowers at the outer perimeter building to large ones at the base.

Figure 8.3 Tulips illustrate rhythm in an arrangement. (Courtesy Pennsylvania State University.)

In addition to repeating individual forms of plant materials, the planes, curves, and lines need to be coordinated rhythmically. Each arrangement should have one dominant line or curve, with each flower stem contributing to the envisioned form, and no opposite movement to interrupt the rhythm.

As with most of the principles of design, the importance of rhythm varies from arrangement to arrangement. The Hogarth or S-curve line of beauty provides a great deal of rhythm, while a strict vertical or horizontal line arrangement offers much less.

REPETITION

Repetition of one or more elements in the composition can add movement and continuity to a flower arrangement. This can be done by repeating form, texture, color, shape, or flower, leaf, pine cone, candle, etc. Repetition must not be done in too methodical a manner, or we will risk monotony. Repetition in a random fashion, or a more natural manner, is better. If too many different elements are used, the composition will lose its pleasing effect and be too "busy." Repetition must be done in a tasteful, intelligent manner (Figure 8.4). Without repetition, there will be an undesirable feeling

Figure 8.4 Repetition of hyacinths and beauty berries shown in this centerpiece of tulips. (Courtesy Pennsylvania State University.)

of isolation and a lack of coherence in the design—it will seem like a mixture of discordant parts. One red carnation in an arrangement of white ones strikes a dissonant note because of its isolation.

UNITY

The principle of unity means that all the component parts of the composition should be combined into one entity. There must be an effect of oneness, not of several separate units coexisting in an arrangement. For example, an ununified composition results when all the white snapdragons are at the top of the arrangement and all the red roses are at the bottom. The flowers and foliages must all be integrated. Unity brings us back to design, which is the idealized, integrated composition instead of one composed of separate units. In an arrangement every flower and stem should seem to belong; there should be no jarring elements or parts. The flowers, foliage, container, color, accessories, and background ideally would all blend together as one. For example, the use of white baby's breath tends to tie together or unify the various colors in a Williamsburg arrangement; it softens the discordant effect of so many different colors or varieties of flowers. Baby's breath also adds to the pleasing effect of a plain red rose arrangement by providing the transitional medium.

Unity is easiest to achieve if you limit yourself to a small number of flowers and only two or three different varieties. This also prevents the flowers from becoming crowded and allows them to retain their individuality. Flowers used together should have something in common with each other. Avoid using exotic or unusual flowers with common garden flowers. Unity is also achieved through the use of repetition, as discussed previously.

FOCUS OR ACCENT

Each flower arrangement has a focal point or center of interest to which the eye is drawn immediately upon looking at the composition. This is particularly true of one-sided arrangements placed along a wall. The focal point is the place of greatest emphasis or dominance. It is generally a little above the point from which the stems start, and near the base of the main vertical axis, somewhat above the rim of the container, and in line with the base of the tallest plant material. The greatest visual weight should be at this point, as well as the largest blooms, the strongest colors, and the most closely packed masses of foliage. We make the focal point definite enough so that it acts as a real center of interest, but not so overpowering that the rest of the arrangement is dwarfed. All the other elements in the arrangement are subordinate to it.

Accent refers to a point of contrast in the arrangement, usually achieved through the use of differing sizes or colors. However, accenting must not be done in too precise, orderly, or mathematical a manner or it will appear contrived. There may be more than one area of accent in an arrangement to add interest to it. However, the greatest area of contrast or accent is usually the focal point. Accent emphasizes one or more areas in the arrangement by giving them special prominence. These areas of contrast keep the arrangement from being too monotonous.

Many flower arrangements, for example a bowl of roses, do not have a strong focal point; some may have as many as four or five. However, most one-sided line arrangements do have one main focal point which briefly attracts the viewer's eye and then allows the viewer to explore the other points of interest in the arrangement.

9

Flower Arranging Guidelines

Horticultural shows around the turn of the century were primarily exhibitions of individual flowers or plant specimens and landscaped garden scenes. However, shortly after the end of World War I, flowers displayed in artistic designs or *arrangements* began to become a prominent feature at some of the larger flower shows. This new art form—new at least to America—caught the imaginations of garden club members and spread rapidly. The members of the Federated Garden Clubs of America and The Garden Club of America are credited with developing the artistic standards for flower arranging through their designs, competition, and regulations as published in their handbooks and followed by many flower arrangers in the United States.

Since the early 1930s, the National Council of State Garden Clubs, Inc., has been very active in the establishment, support, and supervision of a program of flower show schools. One of the prime objectives of the schools is to guide and train people in creating designs with plant materials for their homes and flower shows. In order to standardize their approach to teaching people how to grow plant materials and use them in flower arranging compositions, the *Handbook for Flower Shows* was compiled and published. The handbook is revised and updated periodically. The handbook represents one of the best attempts to define the principles of the American style of flower arranging.

Today, in many flower shows the excitement and participation in the flower arranging portion of the show is much greater than the horticultural specimen portion. Indeed, many flower shows are now "billed" as flower arranging shows. The staging, judging, and competitive interest generated by the flower arranging shows has encouraged a broader concern for how floral compositions should be created, assembled, and exhibited.

Flower arranging is not a science, but a craft and an art. Some of the physical sciences, like chemistry and physics, have laws which give rise to certain principles and rules. Flower arranging, as an art form, does not have rules per se, but there are certain techniques and principles which are important to know and which, if followed, will aid in composing an aesthetically pleasing arrangement. Instead of calling them rules, it may be preferable to call them guidelines or simply "suggestions."

These guidelines are not inviolate but have been developed to assist the designer in creating a flower arrangement which is appealing to a majority of people. The student should seek to master the basic design principles and become adept at assembling plant materials into attractive forms.

To achieve a good design, the following suggestions are fundamental, although these recommendations may be adjusted slightly for some flower arrangements. The fundamentals will help you achieve a good design while you are learning; but once you gain experience, you can "give in" to a creative urge and begin modifying them. Until the basics are mastered, and the reasons for them understood, free form designs will likely prove unsuccessful. Here, then, are some suggestions for the arranger:

1. The *height* of the arrangement should be at least one and a half to two times the height of a tall container (vase) or the width or length, whichever is greater, of a low tray or bowl. Height is measured from the rim of the container to the top of the tallest flower or foliage. The foliage which is used in the arrangement follows the same form as the flowers in the arrangement, and may be above the tallest flower, below it, or just about the same height. This depends on the habit of the designer and the way the materials are used in each flower arrangement. Usually a measurement of one and a half times the height of the vase is appropriate where the container is small, or if only a few flowers are used, or if the design is to have a strong base line. If a large, heavy container is used or the flowers are light, then the height may be twice the height of the container, or slightly higher.

2. The total *width* of the arrangement should be less than twice the height. It may be just slightly less or much less, depending upon the design. The tallest flower is most often the longest flower in all vertical type arrangements, or the design will not have the proper form, proportion, and balance. (With horizontal arrangements, the tallest flower in the center of the arrangement will not have the longest stem.) For example, the width of an arrangement which is 15 inches high (total) will be less than 30 inches in

total width. It may be 29 inches wide or only 6 or 8 inches wide, or any width in between. The height and width of the floral arrangement will usually be in the proper proportion to the container if these suggestions are followed (Figures 9.1 and 9.2).

3. Although each piece of material used in an arrangement possesses depth, the flower arranger must build *depth* into the total composition. By skillful placement of the plant materials, the arranger prevents the design from becoming too flat. In order to avoid serious balance problems, and yet obtain depth in the arrangement, the tallest piece of flower or plant material in the design should not be too far from the physical center of the vase (or flower holder when using a bowl or flat dish container).

4. Buds and small flowers are placed primarily at the top and outer edges of the arrangement. This does not mean that some small flowers may not be scattered throughout the arrangement; in fact, they should be arranged that way. Larger flowers are generally used at the base of the arrangement and near the center to

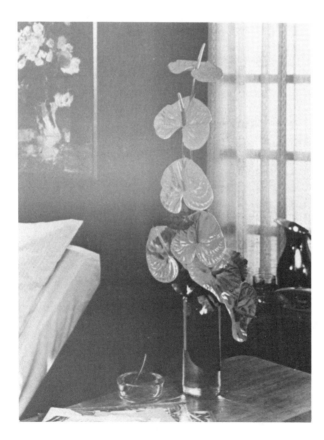

Figure 9.1 A traditional arrangement in a vertical design with composition of materials in mind. (Courtesy Pennsylvania State University.)

Figure 9.2 A bouquet of mixed flowers and colors in the Williamsburg tradition. (Courtesy Teleflora, Inc.)

provide proper balance. This creates a problem for the beginning designer because the larger flowers often have the longest stems and the smaller flowers shorter stems. Don't hesitate to shorten the long stems. Otherwise, you may end up with an unbalanced or top-heavy arrangement. Be sure to vary the stem lengths of like flowers.

5. Given the opportunity, light-colored flowers would be placed primarily at the top and outer edges, while most of the darker flowers are located near the base and in towards the center. Placement of color should be planned in the design of the arrangement. This does not mean lights and darks should be isolated or "zoned" into the design but, rather, subtly integrated.

6. Frequently, two or three types of flowers are used in a contemporary American arrangement. Four or five is normally the maximum. Many people still like the old-fashioned mixed bouquet or *Williamsburg* with its many different mixtures of types and colors. But the mixed bouquets of the Williamsburg tradition are usually much smaller and rounder than the traditional large, fan-shaped arrangements of the 18th century. A mixed bouquet is illustrated in Figure 9.2.

7. The number of colors is often the same as the number of types of flowers; that is, one to three are preferred with four different colors being the maximum.

8. When combining flowers of different colors, select three light for each dark flower if they are the same size. If the sizes vary, then this must be compensated for in the arrangement. The ratio of 3:1 is a reliable guideline. Thus, three white roses would be used for each red rose. However, we should adjust for intensities. Use two pink to one red, or one light pink to one dark pink flower. The arranger must adjust the proportion of color according to the size and types of flowers as well as the intensity and value of the colors.

9. If possible, use an uneven number of flowers. Above 12, the number is unimportant. Most people find that the uneven numbers of 1, 3, 5, 7, and 9 are much more pleasing to the eye. The exception to this is 6 when one receives a half dozen flowers and wishes to use all six in one arrangement. It can be done if the principles of balance, rhythm, and scale are observed and/or foliage or branches are also used.

10. Begin the flower arrangement by placing the steeple or linear form materials in the design to create the skeleton or "bone" structure. If small flowers, like baby's breath, *caspia,* or statice are to be used, place some of them next. The round shaped or "button" flowers are last, and integrated with the steeple and filler materials.

11. Very often as the round or button flowers are positioned in the arrangement, the top and outer edge flowers are placed so the viewer receives a definite profile of the blossom. As the placement proceeds toward the center and base of the design, the profile should be gradually reduced until the focal point flower or flowers are viewed from a full-face angle.

12. Be sure to finish the lower part of the arrangement with flowers and foliages. This helps to hide the mechanics, such as a foam material, and gives the flower arrangement a "finished" look.

The above suggestions are given for the designer to observe in constructing the American style of flower arrangement. Although they are by no means mandatory, it will be helpful for beginners to follow them while becoming more skilled in the art of flower arranging.

FAULTS OR ERRORS

The following faults or errors should be avoided in arranging flowers and foliages in a well-constructed design (Figure 9.3). These faults are mainly

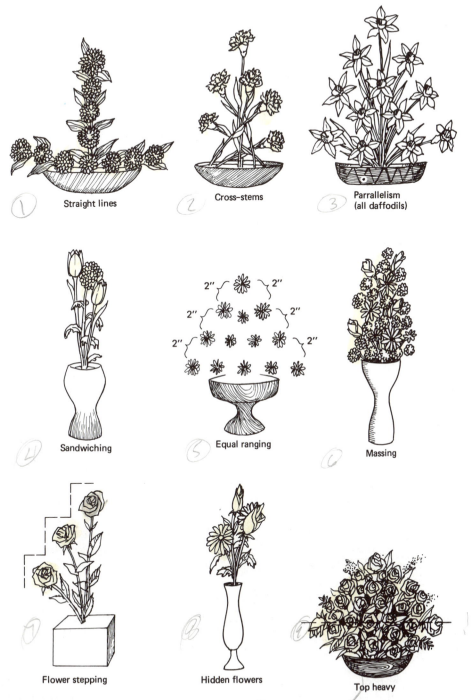

1. Straight lines

2. Cross-stems

3. Parrallelism (all daffodils)

4. Sandwiching

5. Equal ranging

2" 2"
2" 2"
2" 2"

6. Massing

7. Flower stepping

8. Hidden flowers

9. Top heavy

Figure 9.3 Nine faults to avoid in flower arranging.

mechanical errors which occur in the construction of a floral design but may also be those which result if the principles of design are violated.

1. *Straight lines:* The placing of flowers in a straight line either horizontally, vertically, or diagonally. Avoid by placing the flowers in different planes to break up the straight line and develop depth or the third dimension.

2. *Cross stemming (cutting):* The stems of the flowers and foliages cross one another above the rim of the container, where they are visible. Reposition these crossed stems so they are not seen in the arrangement. Construct the design so as to make the flower stems appear to originate from the same place.

3. *Parallelism:* The facing of all flowers in approximately the same direction. Select the flowers and place them so that some face to the left, some to the right, some upwards, and some downwards. For example, 12 daffodils placed with the trumpets all facing straight ahead would not present a natural appearance and would be boring.

4. *Sandwiching:* One flower is crowded next to another, one on top of another, or two or three so close together that they give the impression of a sandwich.

5. *Equal ranging:* Adjacent flowers are the same distance apart throughout the arrangement. Such placement results in a mathematical, monotonous look. Make your arrangement look as natural as possible.

6. *Massing:* Flowers all jammed together into one mass with little or no space between them. Each flower should retain its own individuality.

7. *Flower stepping:* Flowers so placed as to give the appearance of steps along one or more vertical lines of the design. This can be avoided by placing flowers in different planes.

8. *Hidden flowers:* One flower completely hiding another. One rose may partially hide a few florets on a snapdragon, but it should not block or hide another flower entirely; this would be a waste of usable plant material.

9. *Poor proportion and balance:* Too much plant material above an imaginary horizontal line halfway up the arrangement. This results in a top-heavy look. More material must be below this horizontal centerline in the design.

Many of these errors or faults in design are committed inadvertently by the novice floral arranger, but by keeping these suggestions in mind the faults and errors may be reduced.

10
Steps in Construction of a Floral Composition

MENTAL PLANNING

A good flower arrangement does not just happen, but requires planning. One of the first considerations is the occasion. A flower arrangement for a wedding or wedding shower will be much more stylized or "formal" in appearance than one for the home; a large table centerpiece for a banquet will differ from a "homey" arrangement for the coffee table of a friend. It might even be a bright buffet arrangement, say red zinnias and yellow snapdragons, for the snack table against the wall. It might be an all-around or free-standing arrangement to be used for a dining table centerpiece or on a coffee table.

After a place is selected, one must decide what form of balance the flower arrangement will need to fit its location. It will be either symmetrical or asymmetrical.

The next step is to create a mental picture of the arrangement, first by selecting one of the 13 geometric forms presented in Chapter 6. The flower arrangement may not end up exactly as imagined, but the mental picture provides a starting point.

The arranger must then determine what flowers and plant materials are available. If they are being grown in the arranger's or a neighbor's garden, the materials will need to be cut and conditioned sometime before they are used. Flowers and greens obtained from the local florist will have already been conditioned. Care of plant materials will be presented in Chapter 11.

The final step is to select a suitable container and/or mechanical aid such as a frog, flower holder, or foam (see Chapter 14). Often the shortage of suitable containers and/or flower holders is more acute in American households than flower and plant materials (see Chapters 12 and 14 on containers and their use).

Plenty of time must be allowed to make a flower arrangement. It is often difficult to be creative under the pressure of a deadline. Each item of plant material, container, and holder has an individual characteristic and will sometimes resist the efforts of the designer to achieve just the right position under pressure.

Now the arranger is ready for the actual construction. First, select the flowers and/or foliage for the main lines, then the secondary flowers and foliages. If only one type of flower is going to be used, this may dictate the type of container and other factors to be considered. Decide what filler flower to use, if any. For example, the main line might be constructed from white snapdragons with red roses for the secondary flower and a few sprays of baby's breath as a filler. Select the foliage or foliages. One or more foliages may be used but if too many different foliages are combined, the flower arrangement may look more like a jungle than a floral design. The foliages may be either the natural foliage of the flowers in the arrangement such as rose foliage with roses, or a neutral foliage such as leatherleaf (Baker) fern, asparagus, *podocarpus,* or cedar. Avoid using a foliage that normally has a flower associated with it unless the flower is in the arrangement. Daffodil foliage would rarely be used, for example, with roses in an all rose arrangement.

The most important step in making flower arrangements is the construction of the basic skeleton, based on the geometric form chosen for the design. Make sure all parts of the skeleton, and indeed the entire arrangement, conform to this basic shape.

CONSTRUCTION

Constructing a Vertical (Upright) Arrangement

The seven steps given below are essential in the construction of vertical or upright arrangements using symmetrical triangle, asymmetrical triangle, L triangle, vertical, oval, round, spiral, diagonal, and Hogarth curve design forms:

> *Step one:* Put water in the container. This will be plain (unsoftened) water, plus a preservative if needlepoint holder, chicken wire, or shredded styrofoam is used (see Chapter 11 for preservatives and Chapter 14 for holders). If using a water-absorbing plastic foam such as Oasis, Filfast, Viva, Floralife, or Ole', be sure the foam is well-

The Design / Part II

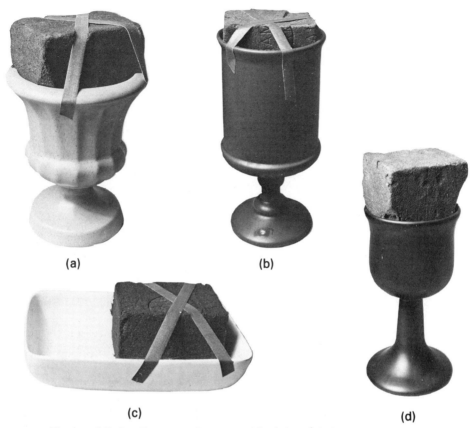

(a)　　　　　　　　　　(b)

(c)　　　　　　　　　　(d)

Figure 10.1 Constructing a vertical (upright) arrangement. *Step one:* place foam in a container. (a) and (b) Secure foam where necessary; (c) construction of an L-shaped (right-angled) triangle; (d) construction of an asymmetrical triangle. (Courtesy Pennsylvania State University.)

soaked, preferably in a preservative solution. When using a foam that completely fills the container, cut a "V" down the back of the foam for adding water daily to the arrangement (Figure 10.1).

Step two: Establish the *main line* (Figure 10.2). Put in the tallest flower and/or foliage. This should be one and a half to two times the height of the vase or width or length (whichever is longest) of a tray or low bowl. Measure the height from the rim of the container to the top of the tallest flower or foliage. One and one-half times is usually best for small containers or where only a few flowers are available, or when the plant materials look fragile. The tallest flower in a vertical design is usually the longest and most centralized in the design to help preserve balance.

Figure 10.2 Constructing a vertical (upright) arrangement. *Step two:* establish the main line. One *gladiolus* for the vertical line. (Courtesy Pennsylvania State University.)

Step three: Add secondary lines to establish the width of the arrangement (Figure 10.3). The total width of a vertical arrangement is usually less than twice the height; it may be just slightly less than twice the height or considerably less. Thus, an arrangement which measures 12 inches from the rim of the container to the top of the tallest flower or foliage will be less than 24 inches wide, although it might be as wide as 22 inches, or as narrow as 4.

To further illustrate the use of secondary lines, here are some specific examples. If the design is one-sided and symmetrical, and two flowers are used for the width, both flowers will be horizontal. However, if it is asymmetrical, one flower will be horizontal and one will be partially vertical. With an all-around or free-standing symmetrical arrangement using four main flowers, all the flowers will be horizontal. If the same arrangement is asymmetrical, then one flower will be vertical and the other three horizontal.

Step four: Fill in the arrangement with flowers of various lengths towards the front and back. The flowers should be of different stem lengths so the arrangement is not monotonous. These flowers should not extend beyond the outline of the design. Filler flowers, if used, should also be placed at this time. In a one-sided arrangement, most of the flowers should be towards the front but a few are placed towards the rear to give depth or third dimension to the arrangement. Those flowers placed towards the rear of the arrangement will still face forward. This step is often interchanged with the next step.

(a)

(b)

Figure 10.3 Constructing a vertical (upright)
arrangement. *Step three:*
add secondary lines to
establish the width. (a)
Three flowers placed at
the extremities of the
triangle; three flowers outline the symmetrical
triangle; (b) three flowers
outline the asymmetrical
triangle; (c) two flowers
form the L design. (Cour-
tesy Pennsylvania State
University.)

(c)

Step five: Add a *focal point* or create a center of interest. This may be
one large flower or a cluster of small darker flowers. One or three
flowers is more pleasing as a focal point than two. The focal point
of more than one flower should be in the same geometric form as the
main form of the design. Thus, three flowers for a focal point in a
Hogarth curve would be arranged in a curved line or crescent; whereas three flowers in a regular symmetrical triangle would be in the
form of a similar triangle (Figure 10.4).

Step six: Look over the arrangement and add or remove flowers and/
or foliage. If a filler flower has been used, some additional filler
might be added at this point. The designer may add a few more

(a)

(b)

(c)

(d)

Figure 10.4 Constructing a vertical (upright) arrangement. *Step five:* add a focal point. (a) Two flowers added near the center of the arrangement; (b) three iris create a center of interest; (c) three flowers added near the base of an arrangement; (d) second *gladiolus* added at the bottom. (Courtesy Pennsylvania State University.)

flowers if it is necessary to complete the design, or foliage may be added or removed. The designer should not be afraid to trim any extra flowers or foliages that spoil the design. Foliages may be added around the bottom of the arrangement to hide the mechanics and complete the design (Figure 10.5).

Figure 10.5 Constructing a vertical (upright) arrangement. *Step six:* look over the arrangement and add or remove flowers and/or foliage to complete the design. (a) a finished vertical symmetrical triangle; (b) a finished asymmetrical triangle arrangement; (c) a completed L-shaped triangle; (d) a complete vertical arrangement. (Courtesy Pennsylvania State University.)

(a)

(b)

(c)

(d)

Step seven: Leave it alone! Don't fuss with it. Once the design has been completed and the first six steps accomplished, then the floral designer should stop there and let it alone. Unless one is an accomplished designer, fussing with the flowers will cause the design to suffer. This final step is one of the most important and sometimes the hardest. When finished, stop!

Constructing a Horizontal (Low) Arrangement

The method of constructing a horizontal arrangement is similar to constructing a vertical arrangement, but with some important differences. The most common horizontal arrangement is a low table centerpiece. There are essentially eight steps in constructing a horizontal arrangement:

Step one: Fill the container with water, or use one of the several water absorbing plastic foams (Figure 10.6). Be sure to use a floral preservative in the water to lengthen flower life.

Figure 10.6 Constructing a horizontal (low) arrangement. *Step one:* Place foam in a container. (Courtesy Pennsylvania State University.)

Step two: Put in two horizontal flowers, opposite each other, to establish the length of the arrangement. The size of a centerpiece will be dictated by the size of the table and the number of flowers available for the design. It should also be in scale with the container used. There is no guide as to how long or wide a horizontal arrangement should be other than to keep all the component parts in scale with each other (Figure 10.7).

Step three: Put in two horizontal flowers, again opposite each other and perpendicular to the first two, for the *width* of the arrangement. These two flowers will be the same length as those in step two if the arrangement is to look circular from above; they both will be shorter than the two flowers for the length if the arrangement is to be oval.

Figure 10.7 Constructing a horizontal (low) arrangement. *Step two:* establish the length of the arrangement. Three flowers form the low horizontal design. (Courtesy Pennsylvania State University.)

Normally, a round container is used for a round arrangement on a round or square table. If the table is oval or rectangular, then the container should be also. The main reason flower arrangements are round or oval is that squares and rectangles are not found in nature nor are they as attractive as curves and triangles.

Step four: Place a vertical flower in the center to determine the height of the horizontal arrangement. The height should not be over 15 inches, and 12 inches is better as measured from the tabletop to the top of this flower (see Figure 10.7). This keeps the design low enough to see over if it is to be used as a table centerpiece. If it is a horizontal arrangement on a pedestal container and to be used as a centerpiece, then the vertical flower can be of varying height depending on the scale of the design and the number of flowers with which the designer will work.

Step five: Establish the four corners of the design. They should not exceed the imaginary circular or oval line as seen from above.

Step six: Fill in with flowers and foliages, particularly around the base, to finish the design and hide as much of the mechanics as possible. The flowers should not extend beyond the outline of the arrangement. Often a designer will ring the container with foliage first, since it is sometimes difficult to add foliage at the bottom to hide the mechanics once the flowers of a mass arrangement are in place.

Step seven: Add a focal point to which the eyes are drawn immediately when looking at the arrangement. This is the point from which the eyes start to travel along the visual paths of the design and to which they are led back to by those paths. A focal point binds the arrangement together visually, and deserves careful thought and planning (Figure 10.8).

Figure 10.8 Constructing a horizontal (low) arrangement. *Step seven:* add a focal point. A few dark pompoms added for a focal point on each side of an arrangement. (Courtesy Pennsylvania State University.)

Step eight: Critically examine the completed arrangement and improve it by removing distracting or unsatisfactory material or voids (Figure 10.9). Then leave the arrangement alone. There comes a point when further fussing with it can only lessen its impact. Try to recognize the point at which the arrangement has reached its optimum quality.

Figure 10.9 Constructing a horizontal (low) arrangement. *Step eight:* critically examine the arrangement to see if any improvements are needed. The finished horizontal centerpiece. (Courtesy Pennsylvania State University.)

part
III

PLANT
MATERIALS

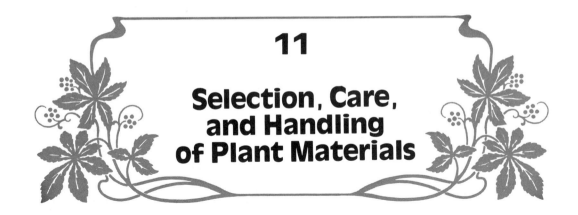

11

Selection, Care, and Handling of Plant Materials

The adventurous flower arranger is constantly on the lookout for interesting plant material and for natural or artificial objects that can be used in a flower arrangement. Distinctive and original flower arrangements are often achieved by original combinations of plant materials. Flower arrangers should always be alert for unusual flower types, forms, sizes, shapes, textures, and colors.

SELECTION OF PLANT MATERIAL FORMS

In general, plant material can be placed into four basic categories: linear (line), background (branching), round (mass), and filler. All four types do not have to always be included in each arrangement; however, it is often easier to construct the arrangement if it has at least linear and round forms. The linear form provides the skeleton of the design and the round form breaks up the space into interesting patterns.

Linear Materials. Linear (line) materials are those which grow into the shape of a tall spire or spike. They are usually tall and slender. Often they are "full" below the tip but taper definitely to a point at the top, much like a church steeple. They are often termed *steeple* or *spike* materials and are usually placed first in the arrangement. Materials included in this group may be flowers, foliage, seed stocks, or branches.

Flowers that have a linear form include snapdragons, *gladiolus*, larkspur, *delphinium*, foxglove, plumed cockscomb, *yucca, buddleia, salvia,* stock, *baptisia,* gay feather, loosestrife, *tritoma* (red hot poker), *thermopsis, veronica,* iris buds, calla buds, lupine, *physostegia, penstemon,* and pencil statice.

Foliages that have a linear form are Ti, *gladiolus, yucca,* iris, Peruvian lily, daffodils, spiral eucalyptus, *podocarpus,* small calla leaves, canna, fern fronds of the heavy textured type, and some evergreen trees or shrubs like yew, hemlock, cedar, fir, and juniper (Figures 11.1 through 11.8). The seed stocks of wheat, barley, miniature cattail, curly dock, crested wheatgrass, mullein, and meadow foxtail also have a linear form.

Figure 11.1 *Asparagus densiflorus* 'Sprengeri'—Sprenger fern. (Courtesy Pennsylvania State University.)

Figure 11.2 *Asparagus retrofractus*—Ming fern. (Courtesy Pennsylvania State University.)

Figure 11.3 *Asparagus setaceus*—plumosa fern. (Courtesy Pennsylvania State University.)

Figure 11.4 *Dryopteris erythrosora* — leatherleaf or 'Baker' fern. (Courtesy Pennsylvania State University.)

Figure 11.5 *Cordiline terminalis*—Ti leaf. (Courtesy Pennsylvania State University.)

Figure 11.6 *Eucalyptus pulvervlenta* — spiral eucalyptus. (Courtesy Pennsylvania State University.)

Figure 11.7 *Podocarpus macrophyllus* — podocarpus. (Courtesy Pennsylvania State University.)

Figure 11.8 *Thuja occidentalis*—western red cedar. (Courtesy Pennsylvania State University.)

The branches of many woody trees and shrubs are often useful in creating the linear form, especially if they are pruned to accent the form. Most outstanding in this group are scotch broom and pussy willow. Others include fruit tree branches such as apple, pear, peach, plum, in bloom, leaf, or dormant. Shrubs such as *Cotoneaster horizontalis, Leucothe* (fetterbush), witch hazel, salal (lemon leaf), mountain laurel, red, yellow, or flowering dogwood, boxwood, huckleberry, and many more are good linear plant materials (Figures 11.9 through 11.13).

The dedicated flower arranger will often indulge in a little judicious pruning of houseplants to obtain a few leaves to serve as linear material. *Aspidistra*, rubber plant, *sansevieria, dieffenbachia* (a green and white leaf), *aucuba* (a green and yellow leaf), and crotons (many colored leaf), to name only a few, all may be intriguing linear material in flower arrangements.

These linear materials are often used to enforce the form of the flower arrangement, which determines its height and width and influences the depth.

Figure 11.9 *Gaultheria shallon*—salal. (Courtesy Pennsylvania State University.)

Figure 11.10 *Kalmia latifolia*—mountain laurel. (Courtesy Pennsylvania State University.)

Figure 11.11 *Laurocerasus caroliniana*—cherry laurel. (Courtesy Pennsylvania State University.)

Figure 11.12 *Buxus sempervirens* — boxwood. (Courtesy Pennsylvania State University.)

Figure 11.13 *Vaccinium ovatum* — huckleberry. (Courtesy Pennsylvania State University.)

Background Materials. The background (sometimes called branching) materials are often used as a partial substitute for linear materials or to complement the steeple flowers and assist in giving additional depth to the ultimate design. These materials often have a greater degree of fullness below the tip than the true linear type, and they are not as tapered to a sharp point, unless especially pruned to shape. The branching materials are not to be confused with filler types, which will be discussed later in this chapter.

Availability of background (branching) material, as well as linear, round, and filler materials, varies according to season and location. Among the background materials available in the spring are: branches of evergreen, azaleas, dogwood, forsythia, flowering almond, flowering crabapple, Japanese cherry, flowering quince, magnolia, and *weigelia*. In summer, larch, laurel, mock orange, rhododendron (many varieties), tulip tree, and *buddleia* (may be either linear or branching or both) are used. In fall, firethorn *(pyracantha)*, fruited crabapple, *hydrangea*, winged *euonymus*, pikeberry, and *viburnum*, make excellent branching materials for your design. In winter, arborvitae, Austrian pine, blue spruce, *Cedrus atlanticus glauca* (which may also be considered linear), Pfitzer juniper, and Japanese yew are available. Flowers with desirable branching habits are pompon chrysanthemums, spray orchids, miniature carnations, garden roses in a cluster *(R. floribunda)*, lilac, *petunias*, regular cockscomb, and many others. The background materials are used to enforce the linear skeleton of contrasting interest to the arrangement.

Round Materials. Round materials (also often called button, mass, or solid materials) are an essential part of any flower arrangement. These materials, usually flowers, may consist of individual flowers on a single stem or a cluster of flowers or florets which have a compact, round, or solid appearance. These round flowers are inserted last in the arrangement to complete the design and create the focal point. Sometimes arrangements are made of only round flowers, but this is recommended only for the seasoned veteran flower arranger and not the beginner, since it is very difficult.

Usually it is easy to obtain the round flowers because there are more kinds of them. They are often the most popular and are found in the annual and perennial gardens of homeowners and city parks. They include the world's most popular flower, the garden and/or greenhouse rose. The second most popular is probably the chrysanthemum, with its great variety of size, shape, kind, and color. Others include carnations and pinks, daffodils and jonquils, tulips, hyacinths, anemones, Japanese, Dutch, German, and English iris, amaryllis, asters, *zinnias*, marigolds, tuberous begonias, gaillardias, peonies, dahlias, callas, shasta and English daisy, crested cockscomb, geraniums, annual and perennial *phlox*, strawflowers, *calendulas*, and many more (Table 11-1).

Table 11-1 *A partial list of annual and perennial garden flowers useful for flower arrangements*

Achillea	Dill	*Phlox*
Ageratum	Dusty miller	*Pyrenthrum* (painted daisy)
Alyssum	English daisy	Rosemary
Arabis	Foxglove	Rose
Aquilegia	*Gazania*	*Rudbeckia*
Astilbe	Globe amaranth	*Salpiglossis*
Aster (China)	*Gypsophila* (baby's breath)	*Salvia*
Aubretia	Heliotrope	*Scabiosa*
Blue lace flower	*Heuchera* (coral bells)	Sea lavendar (statice)
Calendula	*Iberis* (candytuft)	Shasta daisy
Campanula (bell flower)	Iris (many kinds)	Snapdragon
Candytuft	Larkspur	Statice
Carnation	*Lantana*	Strawflower
Celosia (plumed)	Lupine	Sweet alyssum
Cherianthus	Marigolds	Sweet peas
Centaurea (bachelor button)	*Mathiola* (stock)	Thyme
Chrysanthemum	*Matricaria* (feverfew)	Tulip
Cosmos	Narcissus	*Verbena*
Cynoglossum	*Nemesia*	*Veronica*
Daffodil	*Nicotiana*	*Vinca*
Dahlia	Oriental poppy	*Zinnia*
Delphinium	Pansy	
Dianthus (pinks)	*Petunia*	

Filler Materials. Filler materials are flowers or "greens" used in a flower arrangement to obtain a "softened" or "airy" effect in combination with the linear and round materials. Fillers have a fine texture and often an irregular outline. A classic example of a filler flower is *Gypsophilia* sp., better known as baby's breath. Other excellent filler flowers are heather, *acacia, caspia,* many kinds of statice (sea lavender, toothbrush, rat tail, etc.), *stevia,* small button pompon chrysanthemums, and love-in-a-mist. The filler materials are not good design materials in themselves, but are very nice when used in just the right amount to "soften" the lines of the linear and round materials. They are placed in the arrangement after the linear and/or branching materials and before all of the round flowers are added.

THE LIFE SPAN OF CUT PLANT MATERIALS

The desire to prolong the life of cut flowers is a natural one. Whether they come as a gift from a loved one or from one's own garden, flowers at once become a happy part of a room.

The instant a flower is removed from the plant, it is living on borrowed time. Some flowers such as chrysanthemums, protea, and orchids will keep fresh for several weeks after being cut; the life of daylilies is measured by hours; that of morning glories by minutes. This ability to keep fresh after cutting differs with each flower, and it is difficult to prolong that period. However, there are certain methods of cutting, preparing, and caring for flowers after cutting from the plant that will extend their time of beauty.

When a flower and its stem is still on the plant, it is supplied with water by a large root system. The water moves from the roots to the flower through specialized tubular cells in the stem called *xylem*. When the stem and flower are cut from the plant, all the water needed by the flower to keep it fresh and turgid must be taken up through the cut end of the stem by the xylem or water-conducting tissue; the flower is cut off from the practically unlimited supply of water taken up by the many rootlets. Since flowers and leaves give off, or transpire, water all the time, every effort must be made to prevent the amount of water being lost from exceeding the water being taken in through the cut end of the stem or else the flower and leaves will wilt.

Some flowers and leaves naturally give off more water than others and it is chiefly for this reason that some flowers wilt sooner than others. The amount of food stored in the flower and the rate at which this food is used also determines the length of its life.

Drafts of dry air, especially at higher temperatures, will cause large quantities of water to evaporate from the flowers and leaves. Flowers, there-fore, should be kept out of drafts, away from radiators or hot air ducts, and out of full sunlight. Flowers in warm, dry rooms cannot be expected to keep fresh as long as in cool, humid rooms.

Flowers selected in the bud or partly open stage will last longer and have better color than wide open ones. Carnations and dahlias are excep-tions. They are cut when fully opened unless you wish to use a bud in your design.

CUTTING OF FLOWERS AND FOLIAGE

Flowers and foliages may be cut from the original plants in your garden at any time as long as the cut stem ends are quickly immersed in a container of warm water in a shady, protected place. There are, however, two preferred times of cutting: early morning and early evening. Flowers to be used in the morning are best cut the previous evening; flowers to be used in the after-noon are best cut on the previous evening or on the morning of the same day.

When flowers and foliages are cut early in the morning, the stem is full of water; later in the evening, the stems and blooms are filled with sugar and starch. Consequently, noon is the worst time of day to cut flowers.

The best tool for cutting is a sharp knife, especially if the stem tissue is soft or herbaceous. For woody stems, a pair of sharp-bladed clippers may be preferred. In order to expose more area of the cut stem through which water may be absorbed, make a long, slanting cut instead of a straight cut across the stem.

When cutting the stems of some hardwood shrubs (lilacs, mock orange, forsythia, etc.), the basal ends may be further opened to increase the water-absorption area by gently crushing the stems with a light wooden or rubber mallet on a hard surface or by splitting with a sharp knife. This same treatment should be given to stock, chrysanthemums, *zinnias*, and peony stems to allow more water to move up the stem.

Flowers and foliages such as poinsettia, euphorbia, poppy, hollyhock, heliotrope, snow-on-the-mountain, and the rubber tree group that have milky, latex sap require special treatment. Their cut stems must be cauterized or sealed in some way or they will continue to "bleed" and will quickly wilt. Immediately after cutting, the cut stem end should be singed with a candle flame or cigarette lighter for 30 seconds, or dipped in boiling water for 60 seconds, then plunged into warm water. Another method is to plunge the cut ends into a container of ice and water for a few minutes until the bleeding stops.

When cutting flowers and foliage from the garden, place them immediately in a bucket of warm water in a shady, protected spot. This prevents any drying of the cut ends, which could make it difficult for the water to move through the xylem tubes. The bucket should be almost completely full of water and the stems should be plunged to the bottom, almost to the flower heads. The atmospheric pressure will help "push" the water up the stem and assist the natural water movement. Always handle the flowers by the stems to prevent bruising the petals. Use more than one bucket if necessary to avoid crushing, crowding, or damaging fragile tissues.

Some flowers should be cut at specific stages of development: roses after the outer petals begin to loosen; iris when the first bud is ready to open; peonies when half open; Japanese and single types when buds show color. If for use later, they can be cut in early bud, stored dry in the refrigerator at 35° to 40°F, and will open fully when placed in warm water in a warm room. *Gladioli* should be cut when the second floret is ready to open; poppies in the bud stage when just ready to open. Two or three drops of gelatin or paraffin placed in the center of poppy blooms will tend to prevent petal fall. Water lilies should be cut when fully open; place a few drops of paraffin around the base of stamens to keep the petals open. Dahlias should be cut when fully open.

CONDITIONING OF CUT FLOWERS
AND FOLIAGES

As soon as possible after the actual cutting, flowers and foliages should be plunged into warm water of 100° to 110°F as previously described. Warm water is recommended because it moves up the stem more rapidly than cold water. Water movement up the stem is both a chemical and a physical reaction, and both are hastened by heat. The cut materials and warm water buckets should then be moved to a cool, dark, draft-free place for at least two to four hours. By the time the water reaches air temperature, the plant materials will have "conditioned" themselves with optimal amounts of water.

The prolonging of the "shelf" or useful life of plant materials should be started at the same time as the conditioning process described above. Flower preservatives work well. Commercially prepared flower preservatives can often be purchased from retail flower shops since most florists use some brand of preservative for storing their flowers and foliages. They often send out their arrangements using preservatives in the water. Commercial preservatives contain an organic chemical compound, usually oxine citrate (8-HQC), which slows down the respiration rate and prevents stem plugging, delays formation of bacteria in the water, maintains cell turgidity throughout the stem and flower, and prevents fading of colors. The oxine citrate in the preservative makes the water slightly acid. The preservative also contains sufficient sucrose (a sugar) to make the water solution a 2-percent solution. The sucrose supplements the sugars that the flower or foliage can no longer manufacture. It also contains a bactericide which slows down the buildup of bacteria, which can multiply and clog up the water-conducting tubes. The bactericide also helps to slow down the decay of tissue and reduce its accompanying foul odors.

A simple way to prepare a "home remedy" flower preservative that is almost as good as the commercially prepared product is to use a regular (not diet-type) citrus-flavored soft drink and laundry bleach. The soft drink is diluted to a 1 to 4 or 1 to 5 concentration with water. Add about ten drops of bleach to each quart of diluted soft drink. The "pop" supplies the needed sugar and the citrate flavor makes the solution slightly acid. The bleach acts as a bactericide.

Another homemade flower preservative can be made of a little white vinegar and sugar added to the water. The absence of bleach will make it less caustic than the soft drink and bleach combination.

The beneficial effects of flower preservatives can be extended by using the solution in each step from cutting to the completion of the flower arranging composition. By using the preservative in the final flower arranging container, it is not necessary to change the water each day. Just replace the water that is used up.

When the cut plant materials have gone through their first phase of conditioning, remove the leaves from parts of stems that are going to be underwater in the finished arrangement; leaves that are underwater will begin to deteriorate and decompose.

The conditioning buckets and the flower arranging vases or bowls should be thoroughly washed in hot soapy or detergent water after each use and rinsed in a strong bleach (chlorate) solution to kill all the bacteria that are present.

In general, water should not be sprayed or sprinkled on the flower petals. The place where the flowers are being conditioned should, if at all possible, have a medium to high humidity. This might be provided temporarily by sprinkling water on the floor or even hanging wet burlap bags or cloth in the room during the conditioning process.

When cutting flowers from the garden, select interesting material; for arrangements, the largest flowers on the longest stems do not necessarily yield the most pleasing results. Select material to suit a particular container. It is best not to cut so far down the plant that the stems are hard and woody, for these parts of stems will not readily take up water. Flowers should be handled at all times by their stems.

CARE OF ARRANGED FLOWERS AND FOLIAGES

To extend the life of flowers in an arrangement, place the arrangement in a cool room or refrigerator at night. Never leave flowers in direct sunlight, over a radiator, or in a draft, for this will dry them out. The additional heat from sun and radiators also makes them mature too fast. Respiration and other metabolic processes are regulated by temperature and sugars are used up much faster at higher temperatures.

To keep flowers for an extended period of time, store them at 35°F. Some flowers kept at this temperature may last several weeks; for example, peonies cut in bud can be kept this way for two or three weeks.

When flowers, arranged in containers or in storage buckets, are removed from refrigerated conditions at 35° to 40°F, the water should be promptly changed to the temperature of the surrounding air. The warmer air hastens the rate of transpiration from the stems, leaves, and flowers.

Flowers will last much longer in rooms of 50°F then in the 70°F temperatures found in some homes today. Therefore, the practice of putting them in a cool room at night or when not in use is of great value in prolonging their life. Even placing them on the floor overnight will help prolong flower life.

In general, flowers keep as well or better on short stems than on long ones. Do not hesitate to cut off long stems when arranging flowers; cut the stems at the proper length to achieve a well-composed arrangement. It may be necessary to sacrifice a long stem in the interest of design. Whatever the length of the stem, care must be taken that the ends of the stems are in water at all times; in a warm room the water in shallow containers soon may evaporate or the flower may take up and exhaust the water supply, and thus be out of water and wilt.

In summarizing the care and handling of plant materials, here are helpful hints for the floral designer:

1. Cut the end of the stem with a sharp knife, making a slanting cut.

2. Remove foliage from the portion of the stem that will be in water.

3. To harden flowers: Place them in a container of warm water (100 to 110°F), then place the container in a cool room for at least two hours.

4. Always fill a container with water before arranging, or use a water-absorbing foam.

5. Use a chemical preservative in the water.

6. Keep flowers away from drafts and radiators.

7. Do not place cut flowers in direct sunlight.

8. Store the arrangement in a cool place overnight.

9. Add fresh water daily to the arrangement.

SOURCES OF PLANT MATERIALS

The types of cut flowers and foliage plant materials for the flower arranger are many and varied, and availability is determined in part by the area where the arranger lives. The main source of materials for many flower arrangers is their own yard or garden, or their neighborhood (Table 11-2). Nurseries and garden centers in the vicinity are sources for materials, particularly greens. Another potential source around the home is plants growing

Table 11-2 *A list of foliage plant materials available from your own yard (depending upon geographic location)*

Arborvitae	Holly	Privet
Boxwood	Huckleberry	Pussy willow
Cedar	Ivy	Rhododendron
Fir	Juniper	Scotch broom
Forsythia	Laurel	Salal
Hemlock	Magnolia	Spruce
Highbush cranberry	Pine	Yew

Table 11-3   *Houseplant foliages appropriate for flower arrangements*

Amaryllis[a]	Coleus	*Monstera*
Anthurium[a]	Croton	Oxalis[a]
Aspidistra	*Cryptanthus*	*Pandanus*
Aucuba	*Cyclamen*[a]	*Pelargonium*[a]
Begonia, mapleleaf	*Dieffenbachia*	*Peperomia*
Begonia, rex	*Dracaena*	Philodendron
Bilbergia[a]	*Echeveria*[a]	*Pittosporum*
Bird's-nest fern	Gardenia[a]	*Podocarpus*
Caladium	Grape ivy	Rubber plant (*ficus*)
Calla[a]	Holly fern	*Sansevieria*
Camellia[a]	Ivy	*Strelitzia*[a]
Castor oil bean	*Maranta*	Wandering jew

[a]Some of them may also provide flowers.

in windows and porch boxes. Even some of the arranger's houseplants could be selectively trimmed and cut and be used in a flower arrangement (Table 11-3).

The woods and fields are excellent sources for flowers, foliages, and berries. Flower arrangers should learn to keep their eyes open for different types of materials (Tables 11-4 and 11-5).

A continuous supply of flower and foliage materials can be obtained from retail flower shops (Table 11-6). These shops cannot only supply fresh seasonal flowers and foliages, but are a good source of containers, driftwood, manzanita branches, and permanent (polyethylene and silk) materials.

The various asparagus ferns are useful as leafy filler materials as well as to finish the base of the arrangement (see Figures 11.1 through 11.3). Boxwood is a fuller filler used to fill in the background. The leather leaf or Baker fern is the most popular foliage for use in flower arrangements as background, filler, and to finish around the base and hide your mechanics

Table 11-4   *Materials available from the woods and fields*

Cattails	Mustard	Thistle
Dock	Pussy willow	Water hyacinth
Goldenrod	Queen Ann's lace	Water lilies
Grasses	Reeds	Wild aster
Milkweed pods	Teasel	Yarrow

Table 11-5   *Berries useful in flower arrangements, with their colors*

Barberry–red/orange	Holly–red or yellow
Bayberry–gray	Mountain ash–orange/red
Bittersweet–orange	*Pyracantha*–red/orange
Dogwood–red or white	*Viburnum*–red, blue, or black

Table 11-6 *A list of foliage materials available from most retail florist shops*

Asparagus plumosus	Eucalyptus	*Pittosporum*
Asparagus setaceous	Holly	*Podocarpus*
Asparagus sprengeri	Huckleberry	Red huckleberry
Baker fern (leatherleaf)	Juniper	Rhododendron
Cocculus	Laurel	Salal
Coffee	*Mahonia*	Ti leaves
Croton	Myrtle	Western red cedar

(see Figure 11.4). The Ti leaves and spiral eucalyptus are useful to give height and width to the design (see Figures 11.5 and 11.6). Red cedar, salal, cherry laurel and huckleberry help to fill in the background of the arrangement (see Figures 11.8, 11.9, 11.11, and 11.13), while *podocarpus* and mountain laurel are excellent to use all through the arrangement to fill in spaces and provide a background for the flowers (see Figures 11.7 and 11.10).

The houseplant foliages listed in Table 11-3 are leaves that will hold up successfully in flower arrangements and will last for a reasonable time. There are many other houseplant foliages which would be attractive in a flower arrangement, but they would not last more than an hour or two after being cut from the plant.

The range of plant materials to use in flower arranging is boundless. There is literally a wealth of plant resources available to the arranger.

A complete list of flowers appropriate to use in flower arrangements would be unwieldy if not impossible; however, other references may be consulted if a more detailed list is needed.

PLANT MATERIALS THAT CAN BE FORCED

Certain woody plant materials may be brought into the home and forced to bloom before their normal season. Examples of these plants are flowering shrubs and tree materials that have gone through a cold period, and require "forcing" to break the dormancy of the buds. Growth of flowers and/or leaves on woody branches are obtained by placing the stems in water at room temperature and keeping them in a warm room (60° to 70°F) with high humidity. The time required to achieve bloom is directly related to the specific kind of plant material used and the nearness to its normal blooming time. Pussy willows usually develop in 14 to 21 days in mid-winter. However, if picked to force growth in very early spring, they require only 7 to 10 days. The closer to their normal growth period, the less time needed. Some common branches for forcing are: alder, dogwood, forsythia, jasmine, pussy willow, spicebush, flowering cherry, flowering crabapple, flowering peach, and flowering quince; also regular apple, peach, plum, apricot, and pear.

These can be used successfully for adding fresh flowers to arrangements designed for the home.

Dutch bulbs such as tulips, narcissus, and iris, planted in pots and boxes in late fall and placed in a straw or hay-lined pit outdoors, can be brought into the house and forced into bloom beginning in late January. A bright, cool place (50° to 60°F) is needed to force quality blooms.

**part
IV**

THE
MECHANICS

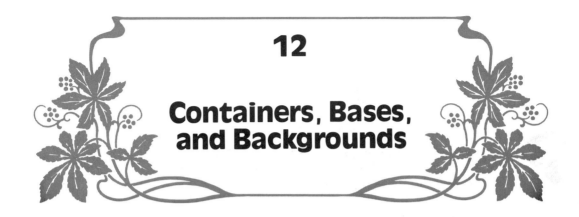

12

Containers, Bases, and Backgrounds

The primary purpose of containers in flower arranging is to hold the flowers, foliage, water, and provide physical support. Flower containers vary widely in shape, size, texture, color, and material. A container can be made of fine silver or bronze, fragile crystal or heavy glass, fine porcelain or heavy, rugged ceramic clay. It may be a gravy boat or a bean pot, a wagon wheel hub or a hollowed-out pumpkin. The main criterion for choosing the correct container is *suitability*.

Before discussing suitability, however, it is helpful to define *vase* or *bowl*. A vase is a container in which the height is greater than the opening or top is broad. A bowl is a container in which the height is less than the opening is broad. A shallow dish suitable for fruit or mashed potatoes is a reasonable example.

Some types of containers that have a pedestal or "foot" are referred to as *compotes* or *urns*. The relatively tall pedestal with a bowl-type top is called a compote. If the pedestal is rather short and heavy appearing, with a more upright or vase-like top, the container is said to be an urn. Often the urn also has a flared top and may have a set of handles or the suggestion of handles.

SUITABILITY

The container should be suitable from the standpoint of scale, design, texture, and color. It should be in the correct scale for the quantity of flowers and foliage to be used and in terms of the place where the flower arrangement is to be used. Scale is one of the most important factors to be considered and often the least understood, especially by the novice flower arranger.

The container must be of the proper shape to accommodate the style of arrangement to be placed in it. If the arrangement is to be upright and spreading, a flared urn is often most suitable, whereas a low oval or rectangular bowl would be best for a dining table centerpiece on a rectangular table.

The texture of the container should agree not only with the kinds of flowers and foliage but also with its intended use and immediate surroundings. An arrangement of roses and snapdragons for the center of a dining table set with fine crystal and bone china would be out of place in a cheap plastic bowl, and would be better placed in silver or cut glass. Pottery with a *matte* or dull finish texture is often better for an arrangement of garden flowers than pottery with a very glossy, bright finish.

TYPES

There are innumerable types of containers, ranging from tall and slender vases to low, broad bowls. Some of the types of containers available for flower arrangers to use are the tall cylinder, pedestal, flared vase or urn, brandy snifter, bud vase, low bowl either round, rectangular, or free-form, cube, and candlestick-holder type. Many of these are shown in Figures 12.1 and 12.2. There are also novelty containers which can be used for plants and

Figure 12.1 Containers used in flower arranging (shown from left to right): *top row:* small pillow, brandy snifter, vase, large brandy snifter, bud vase, fluted vase, smoked glass pedestal; *third row:* bowl, fancy pillow, candle holder, pillow, irregular compote; *second row:* white, green, and black irregular low, flat containers; *bottom row:* diamond, oval, and rectangular low, flat containers. (Courtesy Pennsylvania State University.)

Figure 12.2 Upright and pedestal containers used in flower arranging (shown from left to right): *top row:* fan, bud, round cylinder, large pedestal, medium pedestal, square cylinder; *third row:* urn, large pillow, large pedestal, medium pedestal, square urn; *second row:* small square pedestal, small round pedestal, fancy pedestal, small round pedestal; *bottom row:* lamp pedestal, round flat pedestal, crescent. (Courtesy Pennsylvania State University.)

flowers. These range from a baby cradle to a madonna. If an arranger possessed only three basic containers, they should be a pillow-shaped or rectangular vase, a pedestal vase, and a low bowl-type container.

SIZES AND SHAPES

The sizes and shapes of containers may range from large ones, standing possibly 9 to 12 inches high, to some as small as a thimble. The most common types are round, oval, square, rectangular, and irregular or free-form in shape. The containers may be tapered or straight-sided. They may be wide either at the apex or at the base. The many sizes and shapes available allow the designer to choose one which is suitable from all standpoints, depending on the situation.

MATERIALS

Pottery and glass are the two most common materials used for flower arranging containers. Containers are also made of wood, papier-maché, plastics of many kinds, brass, pewter, copper, silver, steel, and aluminum; indeed, any material can be shaped or molded into a watertight container. Novelty arrangements and miniatures may be designed in a sea shell, thimble, walnut shell, lipstick top, or film cartridge. There is no limit to the materials which are acceptable for containers of modern American flower arrangements. Many arrangements are appropriate to any of the various types of baskets that are available.

Glass is the most delicate material to be found in containers and is suitable for many of our finer flowers. However, glass may also be coarse in texture and thick or thin. Pottery containers also come in many sizes, shapes, and colors. Many handmade pottery containers are excellent for American-style flower arrangements. Wooden containers are especially appropriate for dried-flower arrangements or compositions using fruits and vegetables. Weathered wood, driftwood, manzanita branches, and cypress knees make excellent containers, bases, and accessories for dried arrangements. Metal containers of copper, brass, bronze, and pewter or silver are suitable for fresh flowers such as chrysanthemums or dried materials and various foliages (Figure 12.3). Baskets, cornucopias, and bamboo containers

Figure 12.3 A silver compote makes an appropriate container for this beautiful rose arrangement. (Courtesy Teleflora, Inc.)

are also suitable for various types of plant materials, particularly dried materials. Natural containers can also be used: for example, gourds or coconuts. A loaf of unsliced French bread, hollowed out, lined with foil and filled with a foam material makes an excellent "conversation piece" flower holder for common garden flowers.

COLOR

The color of the container is an important consideration. If the plan is to complement or contrast the color of the container with the flower colors, then a particular color must be selected. However, if the arranger is not going to emphasize the relationship of color, then a neutral color such as white, black, or gray may be used. A green container blends easily with the plant materials.

Normally, the container is supplemental to the flower arrangement. It is not the dominant part of the composition. The container must not detract from the flower arrangement and never "stand out like a sore thumb."

The color of the container may either repeat or complement (contrast) the color of the flowers. The color of a container may be easily changed by using one of the many available spray paints on the market. Choose simple, undecorated containers. Solid colors in muted or subdued browns, grays, or tans are often best. White containers should be used when there are some white flowers in the arrangement, such as a colored *gladiolus* floret with a white throat, or possibly a white filler flower like *gypsophila* or statice. In general, there should be some white in the plant material. The exceptions to this could be red roses or other flowers where the designer wants a sharp contrast with the white container to cause the flowers to really stand out in the design. For example, yellow flowers are frequently best in a yellow container. Any shade of yellow such as tan or brown could be used. Green is a good choice for many flower arrangements. Black is an excellent color for a container because the flowers stand out well against black (Figure 12.4).

Special care should be taken in choosing a container that is of the right size, shape, texture, style, and color appropriate to the place that the arranger has chosen for an arrangement.

Figure 12.4 An asymmetrical design in a black container. (Courtesy Pennsylvania State University.)

BASES

A *base*, as the word implies, is an object placed beneath the container. Many containers, especially Oriental ones, are supplied with bases which are an integral part of the design. In selecting bases that are not connected to the container, the arranger should consider very carefully whether anything is truly gained.

A base is not an accessory, but should be considered as a supplementary part of the container and should be included as part of the proper measurement of one and a half to two times the height of the container when figuring the complete height of a vertical arrangement (see Chapter 10).

Bases may be made of rough wood, polished wood, driftwood, bamboo, fabric materials, stone, "fabricated" marble, slate, metal, styrofoam, reeds, ceramics, and many other materials. Bases are often created by cross-cutting burls or large boles of teak, cypress, walnut, oak, or other woods. Specially prepared ceramic tiles or split or whole bamboo or reed mats are very satisfactory. Utilitarian items such as wooden butter pail lids, or plastic or metal pail lids can be painted and polished to make useful bases. Use a base only if it truly fits into the total composition and is suitable from the standpoint of color, texture, size, style, shape, and design.

There are many reasons for using a base: for contrast in line and form; to reinforce dominance of color, texture, or shape; to provide continuity through gradation of form; to improve the proportion by adding height to the arrangement; to provide visual stability; to promote rhythm; and to provide protection for the piece of furniture upon which the arrangement is placed. A piece of felt fastened to or placed under the base is recommended if it is to be placed on fine, finished furniture.

BACKGROUNDS

Backgrounds are often important in flower arranging. The background includes the surface against which flowers are seen or upon which flower arrangements are placed. The background may be a painted wall, tapestry, wallpaper, or other surface. It may also be a piece of cloth upon which the flowers are placed. Relatively plain and simple backgrounds are frequently the best, just as plain and simple containers are often best. The background can change the whole effect of the arrangement and should be considered as an integral part of the total composition (see Figure 9.2). Proper use is the key. A solid background is usually preferable because a figured or flowery background will often detract from the flower arrangement. The background must fit into the total composition.

Black is a good background color to use behind a flower arrangement because flowers show up well against it. However, it is not always too practical since no one wishes to paint one wall in his home black. Furthermore, although black is a good background to bring out colors, it can have a depressing effect on the overall mood of the composition. For flower arrangements in flower shows, black paper or cloth such as velvet drapes are excellent.

It is a mistake to put most flower arrangements in front of a window. In the first place, sunlight reduces the life of flowers. Secondly, an arrangement loses much of its pleasing effect if the light is shining in back of it. An exception would be an arrangement which has a strong, bold silhouette such as a line arrangement of branches. The branches will provide a strong pattern against the light coming in through the window behind the arrangement and a very pleasing design will result.

A neutral gray-green background is excellent for most floral arrangements. Avoid white if your arrangement is composed of white flowers.

A mirror can be used to good advantage if the arrangement is well designed and properly placed in front of it. A flower arrangement can be made to look almost twice the size if placed just the right distance in front of the mirror. However, if the arrangement is too close to the mirror, the double image is lost. If the flowers are too far out in front of the mirror, too many stems and backs of flowers will be in view and spoil the artistic design of the arrangement.

When using a cloth behind the flower arrangement, avoid loose fabric unless the material is kept smooth. If there are folds in the material, make sure that the lines follow the line and rhythm of the arrangement.

Choosing a background for a flower arrangement in a flower show requires good judgment and restraint. The designer's choice of a background must enhance the design, and not disturb the unity of the whole composition. Backgrounds should be without a crease, winkle, water mark, spot, stain, or fading.

When considering a covering on the top of a table as a background, the same principles apply. For example, an arrangement of yellow daffodils on a yellow tablecloth will lack enough contrast to be effective. Similarly, we would not place an arrangement of yellow flowers in front of the gold pipes of the organ in a church.

The lighting of the background will cause the arrangement to stand out or fade, depending upon how it is used. Lighting behind the flowers, called *backlighting*, will give an effect that varies with the flowers used. A light placed in front of an arrangement or branches may cast a very attractive shadow against the wall.

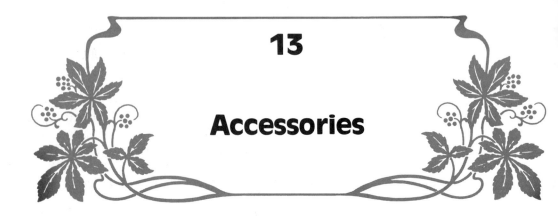

13

Accessories

An *accessory* is any object included in the composition in addition to the plant material, container, base, background, or mechanics. It is subordinate to the design and supplemental to the theme. It may be any object which fits the theme or idea of the floral arrangement. The most skillful arrangers usually suggest the theme through expressive plant materials and containers, and use an accessory to add interest to the arrangement. The overall result should be harmonious in spirit as well as in color, texture, form, design, and scale. Among the more common accessories are candles, fruit, and figurines of birds or animals.

No definite rules exist for the use of accessories in flower arrangements. Designers therefore tend to use their ingenuity but with the caution that accessories must not dominate. Accessories can interpret a theme or express a mood or feeling.

An accessory should be part of the overall arrangement. It should not be attached to the plant material in the container; a figurine focal point would not be an accessory. It has to tie in with the subject. An accessory must be appropriate to its context.

The use of accessories greatly expands the arranger's potential for originality. Accessories are often used to personalize arrangements and make them meaningful to a specific individual. Objects associated with a particular holiday make a general flower arrangement more timely. Accessories should appear as though they were always part of the design and not put in as an afterthought.

OBJECTS AS ACCESSORIES

Creative arrangers make use of both ordinary and unconventional objects to complement their compositions with accessories which tie in with the arrangement's theme, color, form, scale, and texture. Small sculptures, carvings, figures of birds, beasts, people, ancient or modern objects d'art, everyday objects such as clocks, pens, inkstands, bells, hourglasses, snuff boxes, fans, cricket boxes, candlesticks, lanterns, paperweights, books, jewelry, minerals, ribbon bows, semiprecious stones, rings, rocks, pebbles, bricks, tiles, or shells are a few commonly used accessories (Figure 13.1).

A book or magazine is often used with an asymmetric design for a coffee table. The top of a teapot is an excellent accessory if the flower arrangement is designed in the teapot itself. Two or four candles are often used at both ends of a dining room table centerpiece. But candles may be used in any number and placed to coincide with either symmetrical or asymmetrical arrangements.

A separate flower may be used as an accessory, for example where an arrangement is placed at one end of a low tray container in which "free" water is part of the design. This device is an American adaptation of the Japanese style. The floating of a flower adds to the design and will fit

Figure 13.1 A silver anniversary arrangement with accessories. (Courtesy Teleflora, Inc.)

the theme if the same variety of flower is used in both cases. However, the flower must be a complete specimen such as a rose, carnation, or gardenia; just part of a flower, like a rose petal or snapdragon floret, would not be acceptable.

A painting or mirror on the wall behind the flower arrangement will add to the whole composition and will be an appropriate accessory if it blends with the arrangement.

Figurines

Figurines are the objects most often used as accessories in American flower arrangements. Figurines of animals, birds, fish, and human beings can often be found to supplement the themes.

A figurine must fit the main idea of the arrangement. Thus, a swan would be appropriate in a flower arrangement which has motion to it. A small figurine of a medical doctor might be used in an arrangement to celebrate the doctor's opening of a new office.

Fitting the theme should not be carried to questionable extremes. Thus, we would hardly use a small skunk (even though he is cute) in with the gardenia flowers just because they both have a "fragrance" of sorts.

If a figurine is placed away from the main flower arrangement, it should face into the picture.

BALANCE

Balance is one of the important principles to be kept in mind when using accessories. The symmetrical placement of the accessories must be the same as the symmetry of the flower arrangement.

We cannot have symmetry and asymmetry combined in the same composition. Sometimes this can be compensated for by placing the arrangement off center on the table. For example, a candle could be placed at each end of a symmetrical arrangement. The same two candles could be used at one end of the arrangement if it is an asymmetric design.

One accessory can be used with a symmetrical flower arrangement if it is placed in the center in front of the design.

SCALE

Scale is a most important factor in the use of accessories. A figurine that is too large or too small for the proportions of the arrangement can destroy the beauty of the whole design. (Figure 13.2).

Figure 13.2 Accessories well-integrated in a table setting. (Courtesy Teleflora, Inc.)

In painting the use of accessories is commonplace. Take for instance the picture on the wall in Whistler's famous portait of his mother—it is an accessory. So is the green book on the table in Van Gogh's *Women from Arles*. In both cases, if the accessory had been omitted, the result would have been a less well-balanced and interesting composition. The flower arranger, working with plant material, is at a disadvantage; the painter or etcher can make his accessory exactly what he wants it to be in size, form, color, texture, and emphasis, while the floral artist is much more restricted. It can sometimes be difficult to find a physical object that will suit the composition.

OTHER CONCERNS

Accessories can add a new dimension to a design, so it needs to be evaluated in much the same manner as the flower design itself—with attention to the art elements and principles of design. Balance and scale have already been discussed. The designer must also be concerned with the effect of an accessory on the color, texture, harmony, and unity of the composition. The use of an accessory often provides the opportunity to "pick up" a color or colors used in an arrangement and, through repetition, gain additional emphasis and interest. The arranger should also decide what advantage may be gained by using either an analogous or complementary color scheme in the accessory. *Harmony* is the key.

The above concerns about color also apply to texture. It is usually easier to find the color of the accessory than to find just the right texture. The arranger will indeed be fortunate to find both in the same piece, but it is well worth the effort if he or she succeeds.

A flower arrangement often follows a basic theme or idea. The use of daffodils with pussy willows creates a "spring season" mood, chrysanthemums with curly dock suggest a "fall season" mood. A small figurine of a fawn with a spring arrangement or a bright mature duck figurine with fall flowers can provide unity and harmony.

Simplicity is important in selecting accessories. Accessories must not be allowed to clutter the arrangement. On the other hand, any number of accessories may be included in contemporary American flower arrangements. Nevertheless, the designer should not use an accessory if the composition is complete without it.

In summary, flower arrangers should ask themselves the following questions before adding an accessory:

- Does it contribute to the design?
- Does it complement the theme?
- Does it harmonize in color and texture?
- Is it in scale with the design and its intended use?
- Is it necessary to achieve balance?

14

Tools, Supplies, and Flower Holders

A necessary part of flower arranging has to do with tools, supplies or mechanical aids, and flower holders. Tools are used primarily to cut and shape plant materials. Supplies are needed to prepare plant materials for inclusion in the design, especially if they are going to be used for corsages. Flower holders, often called *frogs,* are the various devices designed to hold plant material in particular positions. No one flower holder will suffice for all situations, so a variety of types should be available.

TOOLS

Tools needed for the flower arranger include a knife, shears, ribbon scissors, wire cutters, and a stapler (Figure 14.1). A *sharp* knife is the best tool to cut the ends of the stems of the flowers and foliages. A fresh, clean diagonal cut is made immediately before placing the stem of the flower into the holder. A clean, sharp diagonal cut provides for maximum water uptake by the stem. If the arranger dislikes knives, a pair of sharp shears will do. Shears can be used for all flowers and all the woodiest types of foliage.

There are special shears called florist shears which are very sharp and of high quality. The best ones have one blade with a serrated edge for a firmer, nonslip hold and cut. These shears may be used to cut flower stems as well as soft florist wire and still retain their sharp edge. Some artificial flowers have very heavy stems of plastic-coated wire which are too hard for florist shears. Wire cutters are needed for these.

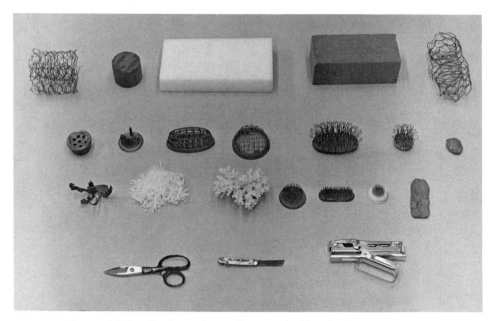

Figure 14.1 Tools and supplies needed by the flower arranger (shown from left to right): *top row:* chicken wire, oasis refill, styrofoam, water absorbing plastic foam, wire mesh; *third row:* ceramic holder, pole pin holder, wire mesh, dome, oval hairpin, round hairpin, floral clay; *second row:* lead, shredded styrofoam, coral, round/oval/round pin holders, plastite clay; *bottom row:* shears, knife, stapler. (Courtesy Pennsylvania State University.)

A stapler is often used to hold the two ends of one leaf together. The tip of the leaf is folded over and fastened to the base. This gives the leaf a ribbonlike effect which is often seen around the base of flower arrangements. Several of these folded leaves resemble a bow of ribbon when placed at the focus of the arrangement. This adds interest to the design, helps to finish the base of the arrangement, and serves to hide some of the mechanics of the arrangement. Other interesting effects can be obtained by rolling and fastening the leaves together lengthwise, or overlapping and fastening several leaves at the base for a cascade effect.

SUPPLIES

Both cut and spool florist wire is very useful to the flower arranger but must be used with special care, especially in container arrangements. Florist wire is soft and easily bent and cut, unlike regular wire. It is available in cut lengths of 12, 18, and 24 inches and also as quarter-pound spools or paddles for wreath making. Florist wire is sold in various gauges only in the even-numbered series. The mid-gauges of 22 to 26 are the most popular sizes for corsage and wreath making. The wire comes both unpainted and green-enameled.

Wires can be used to strengthen the stems of weak flowers in a container arrangement, but should only be used for this when absolutely necessary, and then adequately concealed. Even if the wires are green enamel, they add nothing to the design and are unsightly. The heavier wires are often used to replace flower stems of dried natural materials. To strengthen a weak stem, use a wire that is strong enough to support the flower stem when inserted just under the flower head and then spiraled down around the stem without causing the stem to twist or the flower to drop off or assume an unnatural angle. The stems of some plants such as snapdragons, chrysanthemums, larkspur, and *delphinium* are hollow or have a center of soft pith. A weak stem in these materials can be countered by running a wire up the stem without seriously affecting the uptake of water. This also completely conceals the wire. The thinner wires are used to hold a ribbon bow onto a corsage, to wire very small flowers in miniature designs, or to fasten evergreen materials to a wreath frame.

Two tapes are commonly used in flower arranging. One is the common floral tape or stem wrap used by most florists to cover the wires, forming an artificial stem for flowers in corsages. Floral tape comes in over a dozen colors. With reasonable care, it can cover and conceal any wires in floral designs. The second type of tape used by floral designers is an anchor tape, much like an adhesive tape, which is used to hold floral foam in place in a container. This tape comes in white and green and must be fastened to a dry container to stick properly.

An indispensable material for flower arranging, especially for many bowl containers, is floral clay. Floral clay is used primarily to fasten needlepoint, hairpin, and other metallic flower holders to the container. Less commonly, it is used for support around the base of flower stems in some holders. This is a special type of clay. Floral clay must be used at a time when the container, flower holder, and clay are completely dry. The best way to use floral clay is to roll a piece of it between the hands or on a hard, clean surface until it forms a "snake." Join the ends together to form a circle slightly smaller than the base of the holder and place it on the holder. Push down and slightly twist the holder to make good contact. The holder will be secured by the adhesive qualities of the clay and the partial vacuum within the circle of clay. A quicker, but slightly less satisfactory way is to place a glob of clay on the holder and press both onto the bottom of the container. Large quantities of clay are seldom needed. Ordinary modeling clay is not an effective substitute (Figure 14.2).

Other miscellaneous supplies which can prove handy are colored pipe stem cleaners, twistems, sand, and/or vermiculite (to fill vases for dried arrangements), orchid tubes, corsage thread, pebbles, small rocks, scotch

Figure 14.2 Pin holder anchored firmly into a tray container with floral clay. (Courtesy Pennsylvania State University.)

tape, various colors and widths of ribbon, and several kinds of glue.

FLOWER HOLDERS

Metallic Flower Holders

No one kind of flower holder is usable in all containers. Flower arrangers should have a wide variety of holders on hand. One of the most commonly used types of flower holders is the needlepoint or pin holder with a heavy metallic base. The needlepoint holder consists of a series of sharp brass or steel pins set into a base, usually lead alloy. This type of holder is very popular since it comes in many shapes from round to oval to rectangular, in sizes from a half inch to several inches in diameter. They can also be made into interlocking pieces. The stems of the flowers or foliage are impaled upon or wedged between the pins, depending upon the size of the stem. Needlepoint holders are used mainly in low or flat containers. They do have some limitations; it is very difficult to place a piece of soft or brittle-stemmed plant material onto the holder horizontally unless the stem is taped to make it stay in place. The pins also slightly damage the cut stem end and may make it more difficult for water to move up the stem. Additionally, the holders can prick fingers. When purchasing needlepoint holders, avoid plastic ones which are too light, and those with a suction cup on the bottom, since they often give way after the design is completed.

Another type of holder consists of brass needles on two-thirds of the holder, plus a thick, malleable peg about three-sixteenths of an inch in diameter. The peg can support a piece of driftwood, weathered wood, or manzanita branch in which a hole has been drilled. This permits the designer to use a branch to give height and line to the design and still use the holder's needles to support the plant material in the arrangement.

Another useful metallic flower holder is the hairpin holder, which consists of a series of brass hairpins in a lead alloy base. It is very useful for low, flat containers because by bending down some of the hairpins on the outer edge of the holder, the stem can be "cradled" in the hairpins to achieve a stable low-angle line. There are no sharp points, so neither the plant material stem or the arranger's fingers are subject to injury. The hairpins sit a little high so they may be more difficult to conceal than the needlepoint holder. The hairpin holder is more expensive than the needlepoint but because it is brass and lead it will not rust and lasts for years.

Chicken wire mesh is also a very useful material for flower arrangers, especially with upright or vase containers. Chicken wire coated with plastic or paint is both soft and pliable, and can be cut and shaped as needed. It can be used for many years, and is inexpensive as well. It comes in rolls of 12- or 18-inch widths, large enough for most requirements. Chicken wire can be used by itself or combined with shredded styrofoam. When used alone, the wire is cut and then crumpled and dropped inside the container. Do not make too large or compact a piece because there must be room for the stems. When chicken wire is used with shredded styrofoam, the container is firmly packed with styrofoam and then the chicken wire is cut just slightly larger than the opening of the container. The ends of the wire are bent down so it will just wedge inside the opening and on top of the styrofoam. In this way, the styrofoam gives deep, firm support of the stems and the chicken wire gives stability at the top of the container for support of the more horizontal and low-angle stems.

Experienced flower arrangers find plumber's sheet lead useful for some vase arrangements. A rectangular piece of lead is cut from the sheet. The size of the piece is determined by the container and the number of stems to be used. The sides of the long axis are cut almost to the center in narrow strips. They are then coiled to hold the stems, and the whole device is suspended inside from the inner lip of the base. Sometimes this is called a *dragon-fly* (Figure 14.3).

Metallic holders are superior to the dome, "dazy," or bird cage holders that preceded them. The dome holders had holes that were too large and frequently in the wrong places, and the holders themselves were so large they were difficult to conceal. Ceramic and glass holders were even less satisfactory because of the limited angles they permitted, especially the low ones.

Foams as Flower Holders

In recent years, various types of manufactured foams have been adapted for holding flowers. Styrofoam has been in use for a longer period of time than the absorbent foams, and is available in sheet or shredded form. The

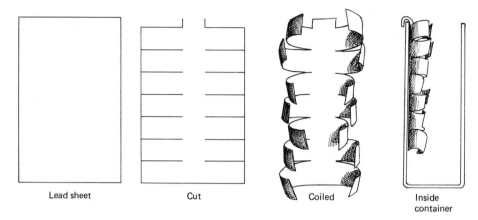

| Lead sheet | Cut | Coiled | Inside container |

Figure 14.3 The various sections of a *dragon-fly* lead flower holder. (Courtesy Washington State University.)

sheet form is used as a holder for polyethylene and silk flowers as well as for dried natural plant materials. Styrofoam can be wedged into an upright container or attached with an adhesive material called *Sure-Stik* or *Cling* to a pottery container. It can also be attached to a wooden base with glue or wire or nails for various types of permanent arrangements. Sheet styrofoam is excellent for use with dried materials, but since it does not absorb water it will not work with fresh materials.

Shredded styrofoam is most frequently used in deep containers with water and fresh materials. The shredded styrofoam provides physical support for the flowers and keeps them in place while the water keeps the flowers and plant material fresh. This material may be reused several times if sterilized with chlorate, rinsed, and dried between uses.

Water-absorbent plastic foams have recently been developed. These foams hold stems securely and are especially good for mass or line–mass styles. They come in yellow, white, pink, red and, most usefully, green, under such brand names as Oasis, Filfast, Quickee, Niagara, Viva, and Ole'. Most of them come in blocks about 9″ × 4″ × 3″ and can easily be sliced to fit into any container. Oasis also comes in cylinders of both 3 and 4 inches in diameter, which fit nicely into containers especially made for that size. Oasis is available in stick and chip forms for use in tall upright containers. Be sure the foam is soaked thoroughly and do not reuse it. Add water daily to all arrangements in water-absorbing foam.

Foams which do not hold water include Sahara and Barfast. Their uses are limited to dried materials. These materials will not stick with Cling, but can be attached with wire or anchor tape. The best material to use in attaching Sahara or Barfast to a board, driftwood, pottery, or almost any container or base is a floral adhesive or glue made specifically for these materials.

The Mechanics / Part IV

Other Materials As Flower Holders

Cheap but convenient materials for holding flowers in deep upright containers or vases are leafy twigs and branches of deciduous or evergreen shrubs and trees. They can be cut up and placed in a vase to give physical support for the plant materials. However, they deteriorate quickly under water and become foul smelling. Glass marbles and agates can be used in crystal or glass vases.

The Japanese have developed some other ways of holding flower stems at desired angles in upright containers (Figure 14.4). Such methods are

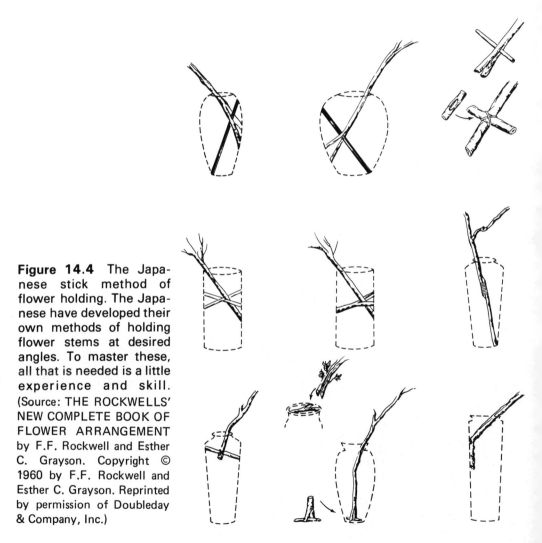

Figure 14.4 The Japanese stick method of flower holding. The Japanese have developed their own methods of holding flower stems at desired angles. To master these, all that is needed is a little experience and skill. (Source: THE ROCKWELLS' NEW COMPLETE BOOK OF FLOWER ARRANGEMENT by F.F. Rockwell and Esther C. Grayson. Copyright © 1960 by F.F. Rockwell and Esther C. Grayson. Reprinted by permission of Doubleday & Company, Inc.)

especially useful for line arrangements where only a few stems are used: a combination of crossed sticks bound together at the crossing, or forked sticks wedged inside the opening of the upright container below the top edge and at the right level. If a single stem of woody plant material is to be used in a vase, the stem can be forced into a cleft of a partially split stick placed snuggly across the container below eye level. This technique requires experience, skill, and patience.

A holder should not be easily visible to the observer. A strategically placed leaf or stem may be enough to conceal the support or holder. Be careful to avoid cluttering up the arrangement. Sometimes a small, clean piece of moss or a handful of washed pebbles or rocks can not only conceal the holder but also add interest and visual weight to the design.

part
V

FLOWER ARRANGEMENTS IN THE HOME AND CHURCH

15

Fresh Flower Arrangements for the Home

In American homes today, flower arrangements may be found in any room. This is distinctly the American style. Flowers can be found in the home at any time of the year and vary seasonally. The living and dining rooms are the most popular locations, although the latest trend is to see more flower arrangements in the kitchen area. When guests are expected for dinner or refreshments, the dining table centerpiece remains popular. Arrangers should let their imaginations run free and place flowers anywhere that seems appropriate. Remember, a flower arrangement is designed to please someone, usually you.

The following is a partial list of places where flowers and foliages may commonly be found in the home; there are many others.

1. *Entrance Hall*
   Table along the wall
   Telephone stand
   In front of mirror
   Vase in tall stand at foot of stairs
   Glass shelves around door
2. *Living Room*
   Coffee table
   End tables
   Bridge or luncheon table
   Piano
   T.V. (permanent arrangement preferable)

Mantel (see Figures 15.6 and 15.7)
On brick or stone jutting out of fireplace wall
Top of bookcase
Dropleaf table along wall
On low table under picture window
On hearth beside fireplace
Niche in wall
New type picture frame with flower holder
Hanging baskets, boats, bird cages, etc.
3. *Dining Room*
Center of table
Buffet table
Sideboard
Corner cupboard
Candle holder
4. *Kitchen*
Breakfast table or snack bar
Shelf or counter beside window
Sink counter
5. *Den* (Figure 15.1)
Desk

Figure 15.1 An ideal arrangement for a man's study. (Courtesy Teleflora, Inc.)

6. *Bedroom*
  Dressing table
  Chest of drawers
7. *Porch or Terrace*
  Table (under glass-topped table very effective)
  Specimen foliage plants
8. *Bathroom*
  Shelf or counter
  Top of toilet tank
  Lavatory stand

TABLE ARRANGEMENTS

Table arrangements comprise three-quarters of the flowers used in the home. Some of these arrangements, because of the particular purpose and immediate surroundings, are symmetrical while others are asymmetrical. Many table arrangements are all-around or *free-standing,* while some of them are one-sided. The use of a specific design depends entirely upon the type of place where it is located in the room, and how the arrangement is placed on the table.

Table Settings

Arrangements for various kinds of table settings and occasions are shown in Figures 15.2 and 15.3. These are suggestions; there are others, depending upon the setup of the tables and the flowers. The flower arranger should use his or her imagination and originality and not feel inhibited by strict rules.

The symmetry of the arrangements and the way they are placed will determine the type of flower arrangement designed for the occasion.

Centerpieces

A dining room table centerpiece is a home's most popular flower arrangement. There are various methods of placing the centerpiece on the dining table, and a number of points need to be kept in mind when designing a dining table centerpiece (see Figure 15.2).

The height of the arrangement should be either low enough to see over or thin enough to see through. This usually limits the height of the tallest flower to less than 15 inches from the tabletop, with 12 inches more desirable. People wish to see the persons they are talking to. Too tall a flower arrangement in the middle of the table forces people to dodge their heads around. If the floral centerpiece must be full, make it loose and airy so that it can be seen through. If people are seated on all sides of a dining table, the

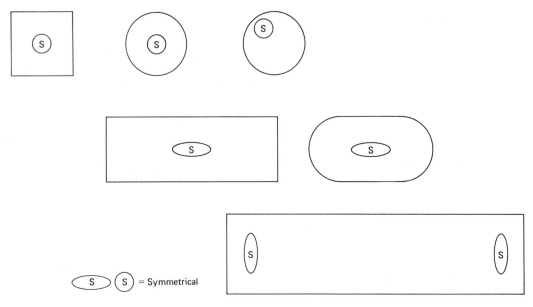

Figure 15.2 Dining room table settings.

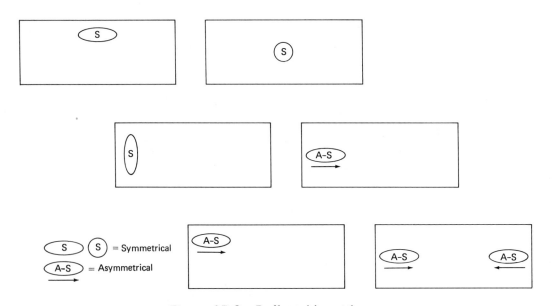

Figure 15.3 Buffet table settings.

centerpiece must be an arrangement which is attractive from all angles. The arrangement must be symmetrical if it is to be used at the center of the table. In general, the arrangement should take the shape of the table. That is, a round arrangement (as seen from above) is used on a round or square table; while an oval arrangement (as seen from above) will be used on a rectangular or oval table.

The color of the flowers and their textures should suit the table appointments, and should harmonize with the cutlery, glassware, china or other place setting, table covering, and accessories. On formal occasions, roses, carnations, snapdragons, or orchids should be used with the best china, silver, cutglass, and fine linens. Conversely, we use marigolds, petunias, or zinnias in pottery for informal settings and occasions.

A floral centerpiece should not interfere with the diners. It should not be so large and spread out that it gets in the way. No one likes to eat a tossed salad and discover a rose leaf among the lettuce or find a snapdragon in his drinking glass. Common sense is the best guide in designing the arrangement for a table centerpiece. Do not use foliage or flowers such as asparagus fern that tend to shed their leaves or petals.

A table centerpiece may contain more than one focal point or point of interest. There may be one focal point which is the main tall flower in the center of the horizontal arrangement. There may be two focal points, one on each side at the base of the tallest flower. There may be three focal points spaced equidistantly around the base of the tallest flower. Or there may be even four focal points spaced around the center flower, pointing to the four points of the compass. It is important that the arrangement appear integrated from all sides with the focus being where all main lines converge. The focus may be accented with contrasting colors or size, or it may be left understated.

The flower arrangement should be in scale with the size of the table. If it is too large or too small for the table, the effect of the composition will be spoiled (Figures 15.4 and 15.5).

Coffee Table

The second most common setting for flowers in the American home is the coffee table.

Points to be kept in mind when designing a flower arrangement for a coffee table are:

- A coffee table arrangement is usually all-around. Most coffee tables in today's American homes are in front of the sofa or a group of several chairs in the living or family room. They will be viewed from all sides so must be attractive from all angles. If the coffee table is pushed against the wall of the room, a one-sided arrangement would be planned.

Figure 15.4 A center-piece of dried materials. (Courtesy Pennsylvania State University.)

Figure 15.5 A lovely table centerpiece with candles and place settings as accessories. [See also Color Plate.] (Courtesy Teleflora, Inc.)

- Coffee table arrangements should look good from above when the person looks down on them. They must give their best appearance from this position since coffee table arrangements are seen from above.

- Scale is the most important principle to keep in mind when designing an arrangement for the coffee table. It must be appropriate for the size of the table and the size of the room.

- The arrangements are usually low, but do not have to be.

Buffet Table

Flower arrangements for the buffet table may be of various types, depending on the placement of the table in the room and the placement of the flower arrangement or arrangements on the table. The important points to remember are these:

- If the buffet table is against the wall, the flower arrangement will be one-sided; whereas, if the table is out in the middle of the room, the arrangement will be all-around, or free-standing.

- The arrangement will be either symmetrical or asymmetrical, depending upon its placement on the table (see Figure 15.3). Thus, the arrangement will be symmetrical when placed in the center of the table or across the end of the table, but asymmetrical when placed at the end of the table with the line pointing towards the center of the table. Two mirror-image asymmetrical arrangements may be used, each facing inward toward the center and focal point of the table.

- The size of the arrangement can be quite large. The important thing to keep in mind is scale; the size of the arrangement must be in scale with the size of the table and the size of the room.

- The flower arrangement must fit with the appointments on the table: linens, glassware, cutlery, china, and so on.

- Almost any container, flowers, and plant materials may be used on the buffet table.

End Tables

End tables may be found singly or in pairs. Here are some pointers:

- If there are two end tables, the arrangements should be mirror images of each other. There will be just one arrangement for one table.

- The arrangements should be small because the use of end tables is not primarily for flowers. The flowers are just an added note of color and cheerfulness to the home.

- The flower arrangements may be either symmetrical or asymmetrical, one-sided or all-around, depending upon the arrangement of the furniture.

Breakfast Table

The breakfast table arrangement is usually small and placed in a ceramic or other informal container. Often the arrangement is made up of just a few bright flowers, possibly from the garden in the summer, or pompons in the winter. It should be bright and cheery to greet people the first thing in the morning.

Luncheon Table

Flowers may also be used effectively on the luncheon table. The style can be the same as that used on the breakfast table. It should be in scale with the table used. If it is a formal luncheon, then the arrangement will be more symmetrical. Also, a flower for each person to pin on may be provided at each place at the table. The formality or informality of the flower arrangement ties in with the occasion.

If the arrangement is to be used on the table for a bridge luncheon, then the arrangement will be very small—often just one or three flowers in a small container such as a small pitcher or one flower spread in a flat dish. It will be a low, all-around arrangement and usually symmetrical. Naturally, the flowers will be removed before starting to play bridge.

MANTEL ARRANGEMENTS

Mantels are a great way to show off the colors and brilliance of the flowers and foliages. If just one arrangement is used, it may be symmetrical and placed in the center of the mantel, or asymmetrical and placed off to the side at one end of the mantel. Two arrangements may be preferred for a long mantel. These would be asymmetrical arrangements and mirror images of each other. The placement of these two arrangements will be determined by what is in the mantel's center of interest. The lines of the design can point either up or down towards it. If there is something low on the mantel in the center, like a clock or nativity scene at Christmas, then the lines of the two arrangements points downward toward that center of interest, as shown in Figure 15.6. If there is a large mirror or painting hanging in the center over the fireplace, then the two asymmetric mirror-image arrangements will be

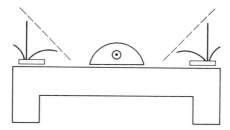

Figure 15.6 Mantel arrangement with a low focal point between two floral arrangements.

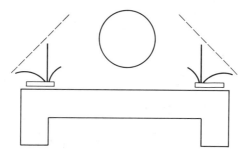

Figure 15.7 Mantel arrangement with a high focal point between two floral arrangements.

reversed so that the eye follows the lines of the design upwards to the painting or mirror, as shown in Figure 15.7.

MINIATURES

Miniature arrangements may be used in various places around the home where a small arrangement is most appropriate. Scale is the most important artistic principle for miniatures. All of the principles and elements of design are followed just as in regular flower arrangements. Tiny flowers and foliages should be used in very small containers such as thimbles, sea shells, walnut shells, or lipstick tops.

Miniatures can be any small arrangement and restricted to any particular measurement. Small arrangements are very appropriate for a bedside table, bed tray, small entrance hallway table, or knickknack shelf. They may be placed on a small table in a small room to be viewed from close at hand.

There are two types of miniature arrangements used in flower shows. The normal miniature must not exceed five inches overall. That means it must be less than five inches in height, less than five inches in width, and less than five inches in depth. The other class is for dwarf miniature arrangements which do not exceed three inches overall.

ARRANGEMENTS FOR MEN

Flower arrangements are becoming increasingly appropriate for a man if the arrangement appears more masculine than feminine. Dish gardens and potted plants have been used for years to send to men who are sick or in the hospital. Now, however, a masculine arrangement of red roses, red or white carnations as shown in Figure 15.1, or large standard chrysanthemums as shown in Figure 15.8 make excellent gifts to be used in a man's den or office.

Figure 15.8 A flower arrangement of standard chrysanthemums ideal for a man's study or den. (Courtesy Teleflora, Inc.)

The use of the heavy chrysanthemums with croton foliage fits in well with the other masculine items in the picture.

There are many places where flowers, potted plants, and greens may be used around the home. They can be used at any time of the year and changed from season to season.

16

Living Plant Arrangements for the Home

American flower arranging encompasses not only cut flowers but also living houseplants. In both cases, the principles of design are the same. Following are a few suggestions for compositions using rooted plants. They are called *flower arrangements* whether they actually involve flowers or not.

DISH GARDENS

Dish gardens are made with small foliage plants planted in soil in a small, low container. The arrangement can vary in size, depending upon the container and the plants used, but is usually small. A dish garden is frequently planted in a rather plain, low, flat container. Sometimes the containers may be a dog, cradle, animal, or other figurine. Many dish gardens are one-sided but they may also be all-around designs.

To construct a dish garden, use a clean container which contains a shallow layer of pebbles, rocks, or charcoal at the bottom for drainage. A loose houseplant soil medium is used and the plants are firmly planted with a definite design in mind. Tall plants are selected for the back (or center if the garden is round) and smaller plants are planted in decreasing height, with the lowest plants in front. A vine may be used to hang partly over the front of the container. With care, a miniature scenic garden can be created. The arrangement should have design, balance, scale, and a focal point, just like a fresh flower arrangement. The latest dish gardens found in retail flower shops are called *European gardens*.

Figure 16.1 A dish garden with artificial accessories added to brighten up the kitchen. (Courtesy Pennsylvania State University.)

Figure 16.2 Artificial flowers and novelties added to a dish garden in a child's room. (Courtesy Pennsylvania State University.)

Dish gardens are grown under the same conditions as most of the foliage plants in the home. Indirect light is best; a dish garden should never be grown in a window under direct sunlight. It should be watered carefully and only when needed. A houseplant fertilizer should be used, but sparingly, no more than once every two months. If salts accumulate on the surface of the garden, an occasional flushing of the soil may be necessary.

Often dish gardens can be made more attractive by adding a few fresh flowers such as roses, carnations, or pompons. The flowers can be placed in plastic tubes filled with water and then inserted in the garden. They will only last a short time, but will be an added attraction for a special occasion. When the flowers die, remove them and the garden will still be a complete design. (See Figures 16.4, 16.5, and 16.7.)

For a holiday or special occasion, the arranger can brighten up the home by placing a few artificial flowers, fruits, or nuts in an irregular manner around the dish garden or even in a specimen foliage plant (Figures 16.1 through 16.7).

Figure 16.3 A living plant arrangement in water (water garden). (Courtesy Gil Witten, Inc., Vero Beach, FL.)

Figure 16.4 A living plant arrangement with three roses added for color and interest. (Courtesy Pennsylvania State University.)

TERRARIUMS

A terrarium is a collection of small compatible foliage plants, growing in a soil medium in a clear glass or plastic container which surrounds the plants to create a humid microclimate. The container may be open to a limited amount of air exchange or closed with a lid. The plants are usually small and compact. They are given only a small amount of soil in order to inhibit root and shoot growth. The soil or some other medium should be no more than two inches in depth, placed on top of a layer of gravel for drainage. Terrariums grow best under low to medium light. Water is used sparingly at the time of planting, and a small amount of water is added every eight to nine weeks if the terrarium is closed. When open, the terrarium will need water every three or four weeks. Little fertilizer is needed as the plants are not supposed to grow larger.

Terrariums are usually one-sided and planted with a definite design in mind. Rocks and other decorations may be used to landscape them. Scale, balance, and focal point should be considered. With the proper plants and care, terrariums should last for years (Table 16-1).

Table 16-1 *Suggested list of foliage plants for dish gardens, terrariums, and water gardens*

Aralia elegantissma	Jade plant
Aralia seiboldi	*Ligustrum*
Asparagus plumosus	Maiden hair fern (*adiantum*)
Asparagus sprengeri	*Maranta*-prayer plant
Baby tears	Neanthe bella palm
Birdnest *sansevieria*	*Nephthytis*-emerald green
Boxwood	*Nephthytis*-green gold
Chinese evergreen *(aglaonema)*	*Peperomia*-astrid
Creeping charley	*Peperomia*-emerald ripple
Croton-gold dust	*Peperomia*-green
Dracaena-corn (ribbon) plant	*Peperomia*-metallica
Dracaena-Florida beauty	*Peperomia*-variegated
English tears	*Philodendron cordatum*
Episcia	Piggy back plant
Euonymous-*media picta*	*Pilea*-aluminum plant
Euonymous-silver	*Pilea*-creeping artillery
Fatshedera	*Pilea*-norfolk
Fittonia-pink	*Pilea*-panamiga
Fittonia-white	*Pilea*-silver tree
Gynura-velvet plant	*Podocarpus*
Hoya carnosa-tricolor	Polka dot plant
Hypocrata	*Pothos*-golden
Iboza	Strawberry begonia
Ivy-glacier	Variegated creeping fig
Ivy-gold dust	Variegated *pellonia*
Ivy-grape	Variegated spider plant
Ivy-needlepoint	Wandering jew
Ivy-variegated Swedish	

SOIL AND/OR POTTING MIXES

Soil or potting mix for dish gardens and terrariums must be selected carefully to insure slow but healthy growth. The soil in dish gardens particularly tends to become compact because it is continually being watered and then dried out. Consequently, the potting soil needs relatively high amounts of organic matter (humus). Commercially available "packaged mixes" are often useful if they contain something more than peat or muck. Perlite (*sponge rock*) is a good additive but is of little value. Peat alone often retains too much moisture, and is frequently low in plant foods. However, it is relatively easy to add additional plant food by using regular houseplant fertilizers and especially the new "time release" plastic-coated pellets.

Householders can prepare their own potting mix if they can get good loam. Soil from a compost pile is ideal, especially if pasteurized before using. Both heavy soils, like clay and clay loam, and light soils of a sandy nature can be improved by adding organic matter. Good sources of organic matter are shredded or milled peat moss, leaf mold, rotted (aged) barnyard manure, and garden compost. A recommended mix is:

Basic soil	40 to 60 percent
Organic matter	30 to 40 percent
Perlite, sand	5 to 20 percent

WATER GARDENS

Another use of green foliage plants is in a water garden, where green plants grow in water instead of soil. First the soil is washed off the roots of the plants. They are then affixed to a pin holder which is attached to the bottom of a low, flat tray container. The plants are placed so as to form one of the standard flower compositions. The plants will grow in the water and last much longer than a fresh flower arrangement. By placing the various types of foliage plants on the pin holder, the arranger is able to make a more pleasing design than with the plants in a dish garden (Figures 16.5 and 16.4).

A few flowers, such as roses (Figure 16.4), may be added to a water garden to add color for a holiday or special occasion. The pin holder should be hidden by using a low trailing plant, larger leaves, or even marbles at the base.

Interest in water gardens is a recent development. Usually the garden has much more design to it than plants growing in a dish garden or a terrarium. A little judicious pruning of some of the leaves and branches of the plants is necessary to keep the plants in scale with the container. (See Figure 16.3.)

Figure 16.5 A living plant arrangement with three iris added for temporary color. (Courtesy Pennsylvania State University.)

Figure 16.6 Artificial flowers added to a philodendron plant. (Courtesy Pennsylvania State University.)

Figure 16.7 Fresh, red *anthuriums* added to a dish garden. (Courtesy Pennsylvania State University.)

17

Permanent Flower Arrangements for the Home

DRIED NATURAL MATERIALS

Flowers and foliages that have been carefully dried to preserve their color and texture are used in many types of arrangements for the home (Figure 17.1). Most of the principles of design that apply in arranging fresh flowers are followed in dried arrangements.

The art of drying and preserving flowers is not new. As early as 1700 in America, and for centuries before in Europe, dried flowers were used in colorful winter flower arrangements and plain bouquets. Lately there has been a sudden resurgence of interest in dried plants. One reason is the increasing concern for ecology. Dried materials reflect a growing desire to conserve and recycle, rather than discard natural resources (Figure 17.2).

The increased interest in dried arrangements has been aided by the recent development of better and faster ways of drying many plant and flower materials. Some of the new techniques involve the use of microwave ovens and of silica gel.

To make a dried flower arrangement, the arranger should select the desired form of design—such as a triangular, radial, vertical, or horizontal pattern—just as he or she would with fresh flowers, and follow the same steps in construction. Since the plant materials used in the arrangement do not require water, Sahara and Barfast are the best materials to use as a flower holder. Some of the water-absorbing foams may also be used without soaking them in water. The foam is softer and the "stems" of wire or picks can be pushed into the holder easier, but it will provide less rigid support.

Figure 17.1 A unique arrangement of dried materials. (Courtesy Teleflora, Inc.)

Figure 17.2 Some of the various dried materials available to flower arrangers. (Courtesy Teleflora, Inc.)

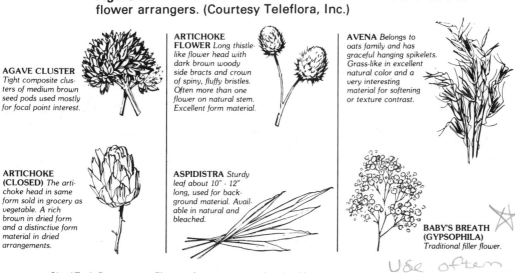

AGAVE CLUSTER *Tight composite clusters of medium brown seed pods used mostly for focal point interest.*

ARTICHOKE FLOWER *Long thistle-like flower head with dark brown woody side bracts and crown of spiny, fluffy bristles. Often more than one flower on natural stem. Excellent form material.*

AVENA *Belongs to oats family and has graceful hanging spikelets. Grass-like in excellent natural color and a very interesting material for softening or texture contrast.*

ARTICHOKE (CLOSED) *The artichoke head in same form sold in grocery as vegetable. A rich brown in dried form and a distinctive form material in dried arrangements.*

ASPIDISTRA *Sturdy leaf about 10″ - 12″ long, used for background material. Available in natural and bleached.*

BABY'S BREATH (GYPSOPHILA) *Traditional filler flower.*

Use often

BANKSIA *Belongs to Protea family. Exotic gray-green form material for line accent or focal point. Head about 5".*

BUNNY TAIL (RABBIT TAIL GRASS) *Dense woolly heads about 2" long used mostly as filler. Available dyed in many colors for use as color accent.*

BUTTERCUP (PUFFED WHEAT) *Very delicate light tan grass-like spike with puffed florets. Basically a filler flower used to soften or blend textures.*

CABBIE *Dark brown in color, solid texture, shaped like a small clover blossom. Excellent filler for form, texture or color contrast.*

CATTAIL *Dark brown traditional line material available in miniature to large sizes; some available with foliage.*

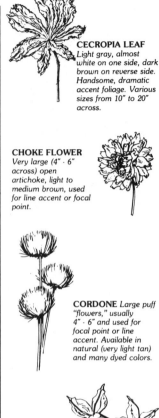

CECROPIA LEAF *Light gray, almost white on one side, dark brown on reverse side. Handsome, dramatic accent foliage. Various sizes from 10" to 20" across.*

CHOKE FLOWER *Very large (4" - 6" across) open artichoke, light to medium brown, used for line accent or focal point.*

CORDONE *Large puff "flowers," usually 4" - 6" and used for focal point or line accent. Available in natural (very light tan) and many dyed colors.*

COTTON POD *Light tan inside, dark brown outside. About 3" across. Available on natural stems for line accent and as individual blossoms for focal point interest.*

CURLED CECROPIA *Very interesting form, handsome brownish-gray color with dark veins. Excellent focal point material.*

CYCAS *Stiff palm leaf, fern-like in form with strong midrib. Usually 12" - 16" long and used for background foliage. Available natural (greenish-brown) or bleached.*

DATE FLORET *Sturdy, thin, light brown line spikes with sparse, snug darker brown florets. Usually 15" - 24" long and used as line accent.*

DOCK (SOUR DOCK) *Long stalked heads, 12" - 24" long, in rich brown color. Excellent inexpensive line or filler material.*

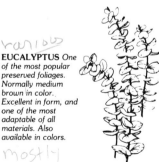
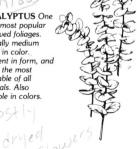

various

EUCALYPTUS *One of the most popular preserved foliages. Normally medium brown in color. Excellent in form, and one of the most adaptable of all materials. Also available in colors.*

mostly dried flowers

Figure 17.2 (continued)

EVERLASTING
Clusters of strawflower-like blossoms, open centers and sparse petals. Paper-like in texture. Open blossoms usually about 1″ · 1-1/2″ in diameter. Available in natural or many dyed colors for filler flowers or color accent.

FOXTAIL Very fluffy light tan spike grass. Good for line accent or to soften and blend textured materials.

HAPPY FLOWER Miniature pod-like flower (1/4″ in diameter) with crown of short spine-like petals. Available in many dyed colors. On single stems used in clusters for filler or color accent.

FANTAZMA PALM
A free-form material for interesting line or focal point accent. Very distinctive, no two pieces alike.

GERMAN STATICE Traditional grayish, fluffy filler used in many arrangements to blend colors or materials and to achieve a soft, airy effect.

HILL FLOWER Small, burr-like blossoms, similar in shape to clover blossoms and on individual stems. Available in many dyed colors for filler or color accent.

FIRE GRASS (BLACK GRASS)
Black-brown airy spike, lighter brown stems. Excellent for line accent, filler or texture contrast. Usually 24″ · 30″ long.

GIANT STARFLOWER
Similar to traditional starflower, but 3 to 4 times larger. Excellent filler flower or good for cluster accents.

IMMORTELLE One of several varieties — this one with tight clusters of small blossoms, paper-like in texture. Excellent focal point or color accent material. Available natural or in many dyed colors.

FLORAL BUTTON (BUTTON FLOWER)
Small (about 1/4″ 3/8″ in diameter), tightly composite flat florets. Normally used in clusters as filler or color accent. Available in many dyed colors.

HAOLE RIBBON BOW (CURLY BEAN POD)
Bean pod-like curls clustered around a main stem form an interesting, irregular material. Dark brown outside, lighter inside. Focal point material.

LIANA (BLEACHED)
Crisp, thick, grass-like material artificially curled for line accent or line arrangement. Long stems.

Figure 17.2 (continued)

LOTUS POD *Dark brown cylindrical seed pod usually from 3" - 5" in diameter. Distinctive focal point material.*

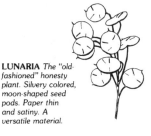

LUNARIA *The "old-fashioned" honesty plant. Silvery colored, moon-shaped seed pods. Paper thin and satiny. A versatile material.*

MAHONIA *An interesting leaf with spiny-tooth leaflets. Excellent background foliage. Usually 10" - 15" long, and brown-green in natural preserved color. Also available in green and red.*

MILO (FEDERITA) *Very heavy grain-like spike 1" - 2" in diameter and 6" - 7" long. On thick stem. A line or filler material. Gives optical weight to arrangement, good texture contrast.*

MINIATURE MYRTLE *A composite foliage for background or filler. Very small leaves.*

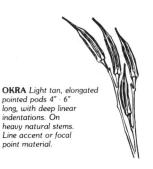

OKRA *Light tan, elongated pointed pods 4" - 6" long, with deep linear indentations. On heavy natural stems. Line accent or focal point material.*

PERUVIAN MOSS (MING MOSS) *Very interesting gray moss. Comes in clumps 4" - 6" in diameter. Excellent for focal point accent or base material.*

PUSSY WILLOW *The dried form of the traditional spring shrub.*

RATTAIL MILLET *Grass-like material with tapered furry tail-like spike about 3" long. Fragile and soft in appearance. Used mostly as filler material in natural color or as color accent in dyed colors.*

SAFFLOWER *Interesting hip-like pod with orange tops and gray-green foliage. Very versatile material for line, filler or accent.*

SEA OATS *Traditional, long stem line material with heavy grained spikes. Available in natural and many dyed colors.*

SOYBEAN (BLEACHED) *Contemporary, exotic material with Oriental feeling. Usually 12" - 24" long with erratic cluster-like tips.*

Figure 17.2 (continued)

STARBURST *Small artichoke blossoms, usually 1-1/2" - 2" across, on natural stems.*

TEASEL *Oval, prickly heads usually 2" - 3" long on sturdy natural stems. Excellent texture characteristics, easily used as line accent, focal point or even filler material. Natural color light tan, also dyed colors.*

WILD OATS *Long-stemmed line material with airy grain-like spikes. Usually natural, but also available in colors.*

STARFLOWER *The traditional miniature single blossoms used in clusters for filler or color accent.*

TIGER GRASS *Looks like broom straw, but much smaller in diameter. About 14" - 16" long and used as line or texture contrast material.*

STATICE (SINUATA) *The dried form of the fresh composite statice that comes in blue, yellow, pink, lavender, rose, etc. Can be stem dyed while fresh and then dried for unusual colors.*

WOODWARDIA TIP *Smaller fronds of Woodwardia fern usually 15" - 24" long. Rich brown color. A handsome background foliage for most dried materials.*

STRAWFLOWER *Traditional "dried flower" in many natural colors on wired stems.*

UMBRELLA FERN *Miniature fern fronds on stems usually 12" - 24" long. Used as foliage for background or filler. Available bleached or colored.*

YARROW *Clusters of seed-like flowers in natural yellow color. Flower is composite form 3" - 5" in diameter on sturdy natural stem. Can be used as line, accent or focal point material.*

TEA GRASS *Another variety of immortelle, usually available on the West Coast. Blossoms small, single, open centers on airy laterals. Natural color excellent for airy but distinct filler.*

WILD IRIS POD *A very interesting and somewhat rare material, usually available only in fall on West Coast market. Pods are about 3" long and tulip-like in shape.*

YUCCA POD *Open light brown seed pods about 2" in diameter, 2" long. Clusters of several pods on short stems. Excellent focal point material, texture and form contrast.*

Figure 17.2 (continued)

Instead of putting in single flowers as we do in a fresh flower arrangement, dried materials are put into the design both singly and in groups or clusters. Many kinds of dried materials are very small or have thin stems and must be used in groups of three or five in a bunch. Thus, we might have three clusters of sea oats at three areas of the triangle or, using the principle of repetition, we might have groups of three to five cattails placed irregularly in several different areas in the design. The outline of the form is made with the specimen materials. Clusters or groups are now added in a naturalistic manner and may also be used as secondary materials or fillers (Figures 17.3 through 17.7).

Figure 17.3 A collection of dried materials in a vertical arrangement. [See also Color Plate.] (Courtesy Teleflora, Inc.)

Methods of Drying Flowers and Foliage
Materials.

There are several different methods of drying and preserving natural flowers and foliages (Figure 17.8). The method used is often determined by the particular plant material and its intended use. A month-by-month chart for drying and pressing flowers is shown in Table 17-1.

Figure 17.4 A stylish arrangement of many dried materials. (Courtesy FTDA.)

Figure 17.5 A contemporary arrangement of dried materials. (Courtesy FTDA.)

Figure 17.6 A *special* dried arrangement featuring cardone puffs. (Courtesy Teleflora, Inc.)

Figure 17.7 A wall plaque of dried materials. (Courtesy Teleflora, Inc.)

The recommended time to pick flowers and foliages for drying is in the late morning when all the dew or night moisture has evaporated, or in the late afternoon to early evening and not when they are wet from a rain shower or overhead irrigation. Most of the flowers should be picked when in full bloom. *Strawflowers are an exception.* They must be cut when the buds just begin to open, full bloom is too late because they will shatter when they reach this stage.

Table 17-1   *Month-by-month chart for drying flowers*

JUNE				
Variety	**Air-dry**	**Silica gel**	**Borax**	**Press**
Black-eyed Susan		3-4 (days)	6-7 (days)	
Buttercup		2	6	3 (weeks)
Coral bells		2	5-7	3
Daisy		3-4		3
Dock (green)[c]	2½-3 (weeks)			
Ferns (maidenhair)		3	6	3
Feverfew (miniature daisy)		4	7-8	3
Forget-me-not		2		3
Mimosa (*acacia*)	2½-3			
Pansy[d]		3-5	7-9	3
Peony		4-5		
Rose (medium to large)[a]		3	6-8	
Rose (miniature)[b]		2	5	
Viola		2-4	6-7	3
Wild carrot (white)		2-4		3
Yarrow[d]	2½-3	2		
JULY				
Ageratum (small blue floss)		2-3 (days)		
Bachelor's button		3	6-7 (days)	
Delphinium		4	8-9	3 (weeks)
Dock (pinkish-green stage)[c]	2½-3 (weeks)			
Dusty miller (leaves and stems)	2½-3	3		3
Globe amaranth (pink shades)	2½-3			
Marigold (small)		4	8	
Marigold (large)		7-8		
Oats (green stage)	2½-3			
Queen Anne's lace[c]	2½-3	2-4	6-7	3
Scotch broom	2½-3			
Shasta daisy		4-5		3
Verbena		3		
Zinnia (small or medium)		4-5	7-9	

Table 17-1 con't

AUGUST				
Artemisia (grayish shrub)	2½-3 (weeks)			3 (weeks)
Cattail[e]	2½-3			
Dahlia (pompon and dwarf varieties)		3-5 (days)	6-8 (days)	
Dock (rust-brown stage)[e]	2½-3			
Goldenrod[e]	2½-3			3
Honesty ("silver dollars")[c]	2½-3			
Hydrangea (green heads of shrub)	2½-3	4		3
Hydrangea (blue-pink heads of shrub)	2½-3	4	9	3
Oats (beige)	2½-3			
Pearly everlasting	2½-3			
Reed grass	2½-3			3
Salvia (blue)	2½-3			
Statice	2½-3			
Strawflowers	2½-3			
Tansy (yellow)	2½-3			
Thistle (lavender)[e]	2½-3	2		
Wheat	2½-3			
Yarrow (yellow)[e]	2½-3			

SEPTEMBER				
Baby's breath	2½-3 (weeks)	4-5 (days)	9-10 (days)	3 (weeks)
Bells of Ireland	2½-3	5		
Bittersweet	2½-3			
Chinese lanterns	2½-3			
Cockscomb (P.G.)	2½-3			
Hydrangea (shrub)	2½-3			3
Pampas grasses	2½-3			
Teasel (brown thistle)	2½-3			

[a] Best varieties are Queen Elizabeth, Peace, Talisman, Pink Dawn, Tropicana, Proud Land (dark red roses tend to dry a dull black).
[b] Best varieties are Fairy and Sweetheart.
[c] Remove thin outer covering from both sides of blossom after drying.
[d] Keep under glass to prevent from absorbing moisture from the air and discoloring.
[e] To prevent shedding, spray with clear lacquer ("dried materials preservative") or unscented hair spray.

Air Drying or Hanging Method. This is the simplest method for drying many plant materials. Strip the flower stems of as much foliage as possible, put the flowers in bunches of six to eight stems of varying length and tie them together with wire or string. Hang the bunches upside down in a dark, well-ventilated, dry room for three weeks or until thoroughly dry. Mimosa, eucalyptus, scotch broom, and dock can be curved if dried upright, or taped and tied in shape while drying upside down. If dried in an upright position,

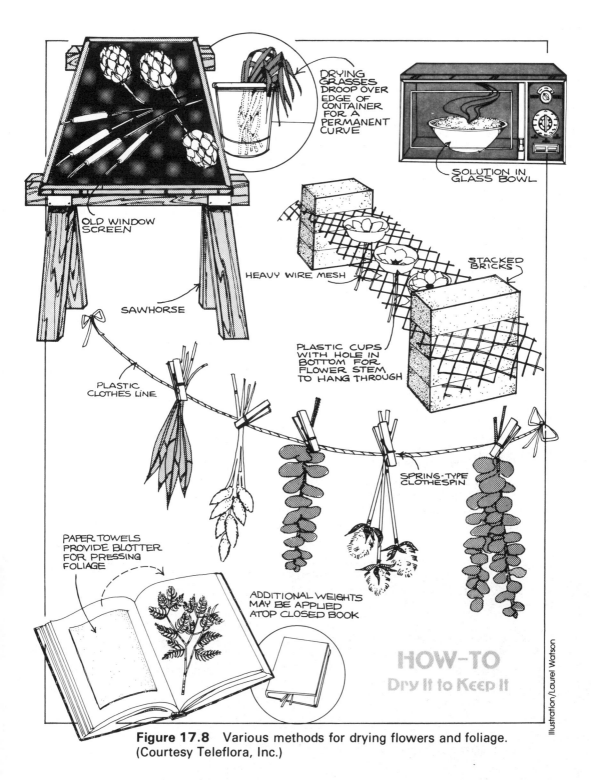

Figure 17.8 Various methods for drying flowers and foliage. (Courtesy Teleflora, Inc.)

some materials will bend or droop in an unnatural way that can be used for very unusual and picturesque compositions.

Natural Drying in Water. The stems of plant material are placed in a small amount of water and allowed to remain there for several weeks until the material has dried out. Materials listed in Table 17-2, Method II, can be handled this way. Cattails dried in this manner should be dipped into clear shellac, thin plastic, or hair spray before drying to keep them from bursting.

Borax and Cornmeal. A mixture of equal parts of regular household borax and white cornmeal can be used to dry flowers. This mixture can be modified; some people prefer as much as six parts cornmeal to one part borax.

Cut the flower stems about one inch from the flower and insert an appropriate wire into each flower head. A thick stem might take #18 wire, an average stem #24, and a thin stem #26.

Spread a layer of the mixture about an inch deep in a flat box and lay the flowers on it. Then gently cover the flowers with more of the mixture, making sure the mixture is contacting all parts of the plants. Leave the materials in the mixture anywhere from one to four weeks; experiment to find the best time for various flowers. Carefully remove the flowers and brush off any clinging mixture with a soft camel's hair brush. The mixture can be dried in the sun or an oven and reused. Make sure the mixture is dry before it is used, or the flowers will rot instead of drying out.

Silica Gel Method. Silica gel is a dry, saltlike, moisture-absorbing form of silica available at many stores under the trade name of Flower-Dri. It is used like the borax-cornmeal mixture but gives faster drying and more brilliant colors. It can be reused indefinitely. The flowers must be dried in an airtight container, unlike the borax method. Silica gel is hydroscopic and may absorb moisture from the air, thus greatly reducing its drying capacity. Even corsages and bouquets of flowers may be dried and preserved in this manner. The types of flowers dried in silica gel are the same as those dessicated by the borax method.

Microwave Method. The newest method for drying some, but not all, flowers is by using a microwave oven. The flowers should be picked just as they reach peak of growth, or they will turn brown when dried. Use a container deep enough so the entire bloom can be covered with silica gel or borax and cornmeal. Fine sand or clean kitty litter can be used. Place about one-half inch of the agent in the container. Cut the flowers, leave a half-inch stem, and place in the material, face up. Sprinkle the agent gently between the petals of the flowers, making sure every petal is completely covered. Place the container in the oven along with a small dish of water. The water

Table 17-2   *Tips on drying materials for arrangements*

Method I. Air Drying or Hanging
Strip foliage, hang upside down in small bunches in a dark, well ventilated, dry room for 3 weeks.

Achilles (yarrow)[a]	Globe amaranth	Larkspur
Bells of Ireland	Globe thistle	Mullen
Bittersweet	Goldenrod	Pussy willow[a]
Celosia (cockscomb)	Grains	Sage
Chives	*Gypsophila*	*Salvia*
Chrysanthemum[a]	*Hydrangea*	Statice
Delphinium[a]	Joe pye weed	Strawflower
Gilia (thimble flower)	Knotweed	Teasel (thistle)

Method II. Natural Drying in Water
Plant material placed in a small amount of water and allowed to remain until dry.

Cattails	Pussy willow[a]
Grasses	Yarrow

Method III. Borax and Cornmeal or Silica Gel
Cover flower heads completely with a mixture of ½ borax and ½ cornmeal or silica gel. Let stand 1 to 4 weeks. Stems of wire are best to replace original natural stem.

Japanese anemone	Dogwood	Pansy
Aster	*Gaillardia*	Queen Anne's lace
Carnation	*Gladiolus*	Rose
Centaurea	Hollyhock	*Scilla* (wood hyacinth)
Chrysanthemum[a]	Iris (Siberian)	*Scabiosa*
Daffodil	Larkspur	Sweet pea
Dahlia	Lilac	*Tithonia*
Daisy	Lily	Zinnia
Delphinium[a]	Marigold	

Method IV. Pressing
For very thin foliage and non-bulky flowers, press between sheets of paper in a book placed between heavy thicknesses of newspaper and heavily weighted for 3 weeks.

Anemone	Coral bells	Sweet pea
Bleeding heart	Ferns	Violets
Coleus	Grasses	Fall leaves
Cosmos	Pansy	

Method V. Glycerine and Water
One part glycerine in two parts water. Place stem end of foliage in solution for 2 to 3 weeks. Foliage will darken.

Beech	*Forsythia*	Maple
Broad-leaved evergreens	Hawthorne	Oak
Crabapple	Huckleberry	Scotch broom
Dogwood	Magnolia	*Viburnum* (berry)

[a]Several methods satisfactory.

will keep the flowers from drying out completely. Set the timer on the oven for the recommended time (see Table 17-3). After drying, remove the container of flowers from the oven and leave it for the period of time shown in Table 17-3. Stems can be attached to the flowers by taping toothpicks, wires, or florists' wire picks to the one-half inch stub.

Pressing Flowers and Leaves. Thin flowers and very thin foliages can be dried by the pressing method. Place flowers and leaves between pieces of facial tissues or blotter paper covered with newspaper and insert them at one-inch intervals in a large book such as an atlas or telephone book. Weight the book with other books or bricks and keep it in a dry place at an even temperature. If the drying time takes longer than three weeks, the tissue and newspaper should be changed carefully (see Table 17-2, Method IV). Pressed flowers can be used particularly well in picture 'frames, with the composition obeying the same principles as in other types of flower arranging.

Table 17-3 *Drying times for flowers in a microwave oven*

	Drying times			
Flower	Number in containers	Baking time (minutes)	Rotate position	Set aside in supporting material (hours)
Azaleas	Clusters, several	2	Every ½ minute	10
Cattleya orchid	1	3	Every minute	12
Dutch iris (bake 2 containers at once)	1	3	Every minute	10
Carnations (bake 2 containers at once)	1	3	Every minute	12
Garden carnations, pink (use cardboard platter)	Several	2	Every ½ minute	6
Anemones, large	1	3	Every ½ minute	12
Anemones, small	Several	2½	Every ½ minute	6
Dogwood cluster	2-3	3	Every minute	8
Roses, large full bloom (use pyrex bowl)	1	3½	Every ½ minute	24
Roses, medium full bloom	1	2½	Every ½ minute	12
Roses, miniature	Several	1½	Every ½ minute	5
Pansy (use cardboard platter)	5-8	2	Every ½ minute	4
Chrysanthemum, large (use pyrex bowl)	1	3	Every minute	12
Chrysanthemum, single bloom (use cardboard platter)	3-5	2½	Every ½ minute	10
Marigolds, large (use cereal bowl)	1	2½	None	12
Marigolds, medium (3 containers at once)	1	2½	None	10
Tulip	1	3	Every minute	15
Peony	1	3	Every minute	12

Glycerine and Water Method. Midsummer and fall foliages and berries can be preserved by placing their stems in a mixture of one part glycerine and two parts warm water. This method is especially effective with magnolia, oak, maple, and beech leaves and branches. Gently crushing the stems and/or removing part of the bark will hasten the absorption of the mixture. Allow the material to remain in the solution for about two or three weeks, either until all of the natural green disappears or droplets of glycerine appear along the leaf edges. The leaves should be gently wiped with a facial tissue to remove excess glycerine.

FABRICATED PLANT MATERIALS

Before 1950, it was easy to distinguish between plastic and real flowers from a distance of several feet; now the quality is so high that one may have to feel the material to determine if it is a living plant or artificial. This is the new era of permanent (or "artificial," "plastic," "perpetual," "fake") plant materials.

The stems of polyethylene flowers and foliages are formed around a relatively heavy piece of wire that has more "temper" than the soft annealed florist wire mentioned earlier. Regular wire cutters are needed to cut them. Wire stems do have an advantage over natural stems because if they are too short for a particular composition, it is a simple matter to attach a longer one.

Flower arrangements are made with permanent flowers in the same manner as with fresh flowers. The same elements and principles of design apply, as well as the same methods of assembly and construction except for the flower holder. Since water is not needed, the material used as a holder can be block styrofoam, nonsoaked absorbent foam, or sand. Polyethylene plant materials can be washed in warm water and detergent or cleaned with a feather duster.

Permanent flowers are also made of silk, ribbon, facial tissue, and various other substances. The silk flowers now available are of excellent quality. New materials and techniques have been found to give the flowers a very realistic appearance, and they can make a pleasing substitute for fresh flowers. Flowers made of ribbon are more obviously artificial, but in some cases this may be desirable. Fabricated "corsage leaves" available from retail florists make the creation stems with wire and green foliage enjoyable.

Permanent foliages and foliage plants may be used in the home as specimen plants and are also used in places too dark for real plants to grow successfully.

There are both advantages and disadvantages to these permanent arrangements in the home. *Some advantages:* they preclude any allergy problems; they last much longer than fresh materials; they are good for offices;

they can be used in areas of low light and low care; and they can be used in heat, light, and drafts which are unfavorable for fresh flowers. *Some disadvantages:* they often are expensive; they become dusty; they may be boring; they fade in direct sunlight; people often prefer flowers that are alive; and people tend to use them too long (as a result, the flowers may be out of season—tulips at Christmas, for example).

FRUITS AND FEATHERS

Artificial fruits and nuts may be used with fresh flowers in a floral design to add interest to the arrangement. These ornaments are especially appropriate for a table centerpiece or an arrangement on a buffet table. They can also be incorporated in a design by wiring them into a specimen foliage plant as discussed in Chapter 16. Such compositions are especially appropriate in the fall and at Thanksgiving time.

Certain bird feathers, such as pheasant, duck, and peacock, have also found their way into American flower arrangements. Not only are they used directly in the arrangements, but also as accessory and background materials. They can spark up the flower arrangement by adding color and texture, and enhancing a theme or mood.

18

Holiday Flower Arrangements for the Home

Most flower arrangements for holidays and special occasions are designed with special concepts and themes in mind. Situations like these give arrangers an excellent opportunity to display originality and imagination.

Arrangements for holidays and special occasions should be original, appropriate, and tasteful. Arrangers should use their imaginations to design something that is entirely different for the particular holiday or special occasion. Use of various accessories and figurines traditional to the holiday can transform a standard arrangement into a holiday specialty. However, do not substitute topicality for good design; utilize all the principles and elements of design as well as specific materials for this particular occasion in order to create a good composition. Always be sure the arrangement is in good taste and will not detract from the occasion. Massive and garish flower arrangements in the home lack good taste. Following are a few suggestions for materials and designs appropriate for our major holidays.

CHRISTMAS

Christmas is a time when the arranger usually takes special pains to decorate the home. Evergreens are the materials most often used for this season. It is a time of extra festivity and joy, which is expressed in the bright decorations of the season. Glitter, tinsel, balls, and ornaments are not only for the tree but for our American flower arrangements as well. Foliages, fruit, seed pods, grain, dried materials, and branches may be spray painted in white, gold, silver, red, or any other color to suit your holiday color scheme. Silvered materials with red and white fresh flowers look attractive on a dining table with a silver service (Figures 18.1 through 18.3).

More than one arrangement is often used in a home during Christmas. The arrangements should be related by plant material, color, and texture.

Wreaths have been used for many centuries in all countries, and are among the most beautiful and appropriate of all Christmas decorations (Figure 18.4). Wreaths are constructed on a wide variety of frames purchased from retail florists or variety stores, or from a wire coat hanger that is bent into a circle. The purchased frames are usually made of heavy gauge wire or styrofoam. A good frame can often be made from a long, thin bough of an evergreen tree after the greenery has been removed. This is especially true with cedar boughs. One long bough may be coaxed to bend into a circle if it is not greater than a quarter to a half inch in diameter. The ends are bound together with #24 gauge florist spool or paddle wire. If one bough is not long enough, two shorter pieces may be bound together into a circle by joining the opposite ends (thick to thin) of the boughs together with wire. The #24 wire is also the best material for fastening the clusters of greenery to

Figure 18.1 A beautiful candle arrangement for Christmas. (Courtesy Teleflora, Inc.)

Figure 18.2 A Christmas candelabra arrangement for a coffee table. (Courtesy Teleflora, Inc.)

Figure 18.3 *Holly, Holly, Holly*—a Christmas arrangement. (Courtesy Mrs. Raymond Biddle, Bellevue, WA.)

the wire and bough frames. Decorated styrofoam bases and straw wreaths are also popular. They can be decorated with ribbon, artificial birds, figurines, painted or unpainted pine cones, and greens of special appeal for the Christmas season. Some of the materials usually used in making swags and wreaths are fir, cedar (*Thuja*), spruce, balsam, short needle pine, and yew. Broadleaved evergreens such as holly, acuba, and rhododendron may be used where the climate is mild.

Traditional flowers appropriate for Christmas are red or white with various foliages to provide the red and green color harmony. The most popular flowers are roses, carnations, snapdragons, and pompon chrysanthemums (Figure 18.5).

Remember that certain holidays have traditionally higher flower usage and flowers may therefore cost more. Prospective brides who are budget conscious might well avoid setting a marriage date the week of Christmas, Valentine's Day, or Mother's Day, when flowers may be expensive or unavailable. Potted plants appropriate for this season are usually poinsettias (red, pink, white, or marbled red and pink), azaleas, cyclamen, kalanchoe, Jerusalem cherry, and ornamental peppers.

Figure 18.4 Mantel and wall decorations for Christmas. (Courtesy Teleflora, Inc.)

Figure 18.5 Christmas holiday arrangement of carnations, pompons, statice, candytuft, and holly. (Courtesy Teleflora, Inc.)

Poinsettias may also be used as cut flowers in table decorations and other floral designs. The stem of the cut poinsettia should be cauterized with a cigarette lighter, dipped in boiling water for a short time, or, easier still, immersed in ice water until the "bleeding" stops. After removing the excess leaves, the flowers need to be conditioned in water overnight for hardening before use. These precautions must be followed if you wish to use poinsettias as cut flowers successfully.

VALENTINE'S DAY

Valentine's Day is a sentimental holiday in which a novelty container is particularly appropriate. Flowers are a traditional part of this holiday. Those who collect figurines will find groups or individual figures of the rococo period in France well-suited to use on Valentine's Day. A heart-shaped container, one with lovebirds on it, or any type of sentimental novelty container would work well. A glass or silver epergne, with appropriate accessories, is a very appropriate container for the table on this day.

For the older generation, violets in a low composition are still the most appropriate arrangement for Valentine's Day. Today, red roses are the favorite since they traditionally mean "I love you." However, due to the price and a shortage of red roses at this time of year, other flowers are now considered

Figure 18.6 A typical Valentine's Day arrangement. (Courtesy Teleflora, Inc.)

suitable for Valentine's Day: red and white carnations, white snapdragons, white *camellias,* white pompons, and the long lasting *anthuriums* (Figure 18.6).

Potted plants which are appropriate for Valentine's Day are azaleas, potted chrysanthemums, and African violets.

EASTER

Easter is another important floral holiday in most American homes. Since Easter is also a traditional eating day, the most common place for a floral decoration is on the dining room table. We usually do not decorate the whole house and front door as we do at Christmas.

The most appropriate flowers for Easter are spring flowering bulbs such as tulips, daffodils, hyacinths, and iris. They are excellent in centerpieces. Snapdragons and pompon chrysanthemums are also used at this time; the snapdragons fit in very nicely with the spring flowers in a centerpiece. Palm

Figure 18.7 A mixed basket of flowers. [See also Color Plate.] (Courtesy FTDA.)

fronds are particularly appropriate in an arrangement for both Palm Sunday and Easter. Roses and carnations are also appropriate as are Easter lilies, either as an arrangement of cut flowers or as a potted plant. Other flowers which may be used are callas, anemones, and lilacs (Figure 18.7). Lilacs, like poinsettias, must be specially treated if they are to hold up in a flower arrangement. The woody stem of the lilac should be cut crosswise in two directions like a plus (+) sign. Most of the leaves should be removed or the flowers will droop, wither, and die very quickly. The flowers should be placed in warm water in a cool room for several hours to properly harden them before use.

Bright yellow *acacia* adds a spot of color as an excellent filler flower in the table arrangement. Potted plants appropriate for Easter are the Easter lily, azaleas, hyacinths, *hydrangea, cineraria*, and *calceolaria*. Potted plants are often dressed up with a bow of ribbon or a few foliages.

Corsages of flowers such as orchids, roses, carnations, and gardenias are often presented as gifts and worn on this holiday.

MOTHER'S DAY

Mother's Day is a holiday for paying tribute to wives, mothers, mothers-in-law, grandmothers, and great aunts. Since Mother's Day is in the month of May, we usually decorate the table with a light and airy spring arrangement of fine and dainty flowers in pastel shades and tints (Figure 18.8).

Figure 18.8 Four *cymbidiums* for a fine Mother's Day arrangement. [See also Color Plate.] (Courtesy FTDA.)

Pastel roses, carnations, and snapdragons make excellent arrangements for this holiday. Other flowers which are used are larkspur, tulips, daffodils, and hyacinths along with baby's breath and *acacia* for filler flowers. Potted plants which are particularly appropriate for Mother's Day include gardenias, hyacinths, potted roses, *hydrangeas*, chrysanthemums, and decorated foliage plants.

Corsages of orchids, roses, violets, and carnations are worn by the women of the house, while many men still observe the custom of wearing a boutonniere in honor of the occasion. Traditionally, the corsage and boutonniere will be white if the mother is deceased, and colored if she is still living.

MEMORIAL DAY

Memorial Day is a patriotic holiday in which we honor the people who have died defending our country. It was originated to honor the soldiers who died in the Civil War. Memorial Day arrangements for the home usually feature peonies, lilacs, and sometimes bearded iris, which are at their height of bloom in late May.

We are not limited to any one flower at this time, and many people make flower arrangements of roses or any favorite flower of the person honored. In arranging peonies for a buffet table, take a lesson from the Japanese and keep the arrangement as simple as possible. Use a full bloom, a half-open bloom and a bud with peony foliage in a wide, shallow container. It can give an effect as pleasing as a dozen open blooms in one large vase.

For the cemetery, a wreath of any of several flowers and foliages is appropriate. Also, cemetery vases of *gladioli*, peonies, and other flowers may be used. A styrofoam cross or wreath may be constructed with greens and flowers attached to the frame.

The potted plants which are used in the home, outdoors, and in the cemetery in ever-increasing quantities are the geraniums and potted chrysanthemums. Large numbers of these and other bedding plants are used to decorate for Memorial Day. Combination pots and boxes may be artistically planted with a variety of annual bedding plants.

THANKSGIVING

Thanksgiving arrangements should follow a bountiful harvest season theme (Figure 18.9). A horn of plenty or cornucopia is often used for a Thanksgiving table or mantel arrangement.

The designer can use any combination of flowers, flowers and fruit, flowers and vegetables, or flowers with fruits and vegetables. Richly colored autumn flowers and foliages blend together easily for appropriate arrangements in this season. Dried materials may be included. Use flowers for the height (steeple), fruit for a focal point, and autumn foliage for the background and to finish the base of the arrangement. Often an arrangement of flowers and foliages on a breadboard with the fruits and vegetables spilling

Figure 18.9 Thanksgiving, a family holiday. (Courtesy Teleflora, Inc.)

out in front of the flowers is used. Low or flat baskets are also appropriate containers for Thanksgiving arrangements. Swags of dried materials including grain stalks may be fixed on doors and walls.

A few of the representative materials useful for these arrangements are: chrysanthemums; dried materials; oak, maple, and beach foliages; citrus fruits; crabapples, grapes, pineapples, avocados, and banana fruits; red cabbage, peppers, eggplant, gourds, and cucumber vegetables; nuts of various types; and ornamental Indian corn.

Centerpieces of pompon chrysanthemums with colored foliages make a perfect low horizontal arrangement for the center of the dining room table. One-sided asymmetrical arrangements fit very nicely on the sideboard at this time of year.

THE NEW YEAR

The new year brings with it two opportunities to use floral decorations that are festive and sparkling. New Year's Eve is a time for partying and ringing in the new year, while New Year's Day is the time for a traditional dinner.

New Year's Eve is a perfect time to have a floral arrangement on a buffet table. Corsages are also worn for this occasion. Some Christmas decorations can be used for New Year's Eve, especially poinsettias, snow-sprinkled evergreen branches, roses and carnations still creating a nice effect. Silver bells might be used on a styrofoam platform and, if ingeniously done, fixed so that they may be rung at midnight to welcome the new year. Balloons and noisemakers are clever additions for party arrangements and may even be incorporated in the floral decorations.

Flower arrangements on New Year's Day are usually limited to a bright floral centerpiece of cut poinsettias, holly, roses, white carnations, or white pompons. Additional decorations may be used by adding some artificial flowers or fruits to specimen foliage plants around the house (Figure 18.10). Spruce up foliage plants for the holiday season, but do not leave accessories on the plants all year long; they are more effective just for a holiday season.

PATRIOTIC HOLIDAYS

On patriotic holidays the colors are red, white, and blue and these should be included in our floral compositions. One problem is that red, white, and blue do not easily fit into any of the color harmonies. Therefore, two colors are usually used in the flowers and the third color either in the container or accessories. Often, red and white flowers are used in a blue container or on a blue tablecloth. Blue and white flowers may be used to flank two red candles. Accessories such as a toy drum or rocket can be used along with the

Figure 18.10 Artificial fruit added to a pole philodendron. (Courtesy Pennsylvania State University.)

flower arrangement. Another idea is to make an arrangement of red and white flowers and insert a few small flags into it to obtain the blue color while adding to the patriotic effect.

ANNIVERSARIES AND BIRTHDAYS

Special occasion flower arrangements are used for anniversaries and birthdays. These arrangements may be personalized by adding a styrofoam number to the arrangement to indicate the year of the anniversary or birthday. These can be purchased at a novelty or florist shop. The 25th and 50th years will be in silver and gold, respectively. Personal items may be added such as a comic book or toy for a child, a pipe for a man, or a ring for a wife or mother. One or two of these items added to the floral design will definitely personalize the item and make it more special to the recipient (Figure 18.11).

Figure 18.11 A fruit arrangement for a child's party. (Courtesy Pennsylvania State University.)

To be successful, a designer should plan for the holidays and special occasions so that the flower arrangement will tie in with the event. Remember to use your imagination and originality to design something that will really be appropriate.

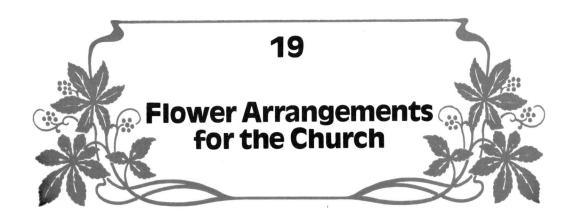

19

Flower Arrangements for the Church

The architectural style of churches varies with their age and location. Flower arrangements used in a church should reflect and complement that particular church's style.

Along the eastern seaboard of the United States, much of the traditional church architecture has been influenced by Sir Christopher Wren, the great English builder of churches. The Georgian styles of flower arrangements, typified by rich, profuse, dignified, and symmetrical arrangements in fine porcelain, silver, or crystal containers are well suited for these churches.

Farther south, the classical Greek revival style of architecture was popular. Graceful vases with more delicate flowers and more variety in treatment of the flowers are appropriate here. Colors will stand out and not recede into the walls of these churches since they do not have heavy shadows.

In the southwest, the use of soft adobe, stone, or crude masonry churches, which is a direct inheritance from Spain, is pervasive. These churches are more natural in color and the windows are apt to be small and high. The light inside is not strong, so both the style of architecture and the dim interior will suggest earthy containers and strong colors and forms. Red and brown earthy tones, or hues of yellow, will be very appropriate.

The midwest developed during the reign of Queen Victoria and has examples of both the simple dignity of her earlier years and the more extreme embellishment of her later ones. Many of the churches show a Gothic influence brought over from western Europe. The churches are typified by tall, slender windows and peaked arches brought together at the top with the same movement as a spire. The stately beauty of an arrangement in a vertical style belongs in churches of this type.

Another type of church found all over our country is based on the Roman Forum. It is almost square, like an auditorium, with the seats arranged in a wide semicircle around the platform, rostrum, or altar. This is the most difficult church of all in which to properly arrange and display flowers, and the one most in need of them because of its size and proportion. Massive arrangements that can be seen from all sides of the church are best.

Many of the churches being built today have a modernistic architectural style. The exterior and interior of the church usually do not follow the so-called traditional layout and thus the interior design may either enhance or inhibit the use of flowers. Modernistic containers and contemporary line and line-mass flower arrangements are appropriate here.

Regardless of the church's architectural style, flower design principles must be kept in mind if arrangements for it are to be successful. The scale and proportion of the arrangement in relation to the church takes on added importance. The color and texture of the composition must fit in with the church interior to be used to best advantage. Well-designed fresh flower arrangements never fail to add a special inspiration to a church service (Figure 19.1).

Figure 19.1 A typical church arrangement. (Courtesy Pennsylvania State University.)

CHURCH CUSTOMS AND REGULATIONS

The first decision to be made about flowers in the church is their placement. Flowers, containers, candle stands, pedestals, garlands, potted plants, or floral materials should not be placed where they will interfere with any portion of the service, obstruct the view of anyone in the congregation, or hamper the movement of the worshippers. Arrangements should be located where they can be seen by all, and they must appear artistically complete from all viewpoints.

In some churches, flowers are placed in front of the pulpit, and in others they may be on pedestals, altar rails, or in front of the choir loft. In some cases, for example Roman Catholic churches, there are only limited choices. The priest of the church will often direct the placement of flowers. Some churches have just one or two special places for flowers, so there may be little choice. In most Protestant churches, flowers are placed on special pedestals or often in various parts of the church. Some of the more modern churches have shelves built out from the walls to hold flower arrangements.

Many churches have matched pairs of containers which are placed together on the altar. This means the arrangements will be mirror images of each other. They may both be symmetrical or they may both be asymmetrical, depending upon the wishes of the designer or church officer in charge of flowers for the service.

Regulations are often changed for a special holiday, or they may be adjusted from year to year. During the special seasons, plants such as poinsettias are used at Christmas and Easter lilies on Easter Sunday.

It is not worthwhile to give specific examples since each church has its own customs and regulations. Flower arrangers should first acquaint themselves with these requirements so as to avoid problems.

CHURCH CONTAINERS

In the formal Georgian-type church common in New England, the most suitable container is the urn-shaped vase. The vase can be tall and slender, or low and broad, but it always has a pedestal-type base. The vase may be made of any of a number of materials like marble, alabaster, pottery, wrought iron, bronze, pewter, or copper.

In the southwest, the rounded Mexican vase, plain and low to medium height, is well suited to an adobe-type church. Brass, copper, and pewter may also be found in these churches.

In the Gothic-style churches, appropriate flower arrangments are in tall, graceful, pedestal urns of marble, silver, brass, or pottery. The vertical type of an arrangement gives a feeling of lifting to the heavens.

In the Roman Forum-type churches found throughout the United

States, most of the containers for flower arrangements are of a size and shape best suited to that particular church. Various materials may be used for the container, in accordance with the setting. Most containers are flared out at the top so as to get the greatest spread possible with the flowers.

One inevitable test to apply to any container is: does the container command more attention than the flowers it contains? If so, it should not be used. The container, like clothing for a person, is intended first of all to point up and present the beauty of its contents. It is a means to an end, not the end in itself. It must remain an accessory, and not become the center of interest.

The next consideration given to containers should concern their style. They should agree with the general architectural feeling of the church.

A container must have a firm base so that it will appear steady and secure and also be weighty enough to hold a large arrangement of plant material. It must have a mouth large enough to hold quantities of flowers. No matter how much water capacity it has, if it is narrow at the neck the stems will be crushed and the flowers in it will soon become a sorry sight. A container should narrow slightly at the neck, however, to support the stems and not allow them to slump in all directions.

FACTORS FOR CHURCH PLACEMENT

In placing flowers and greens in the church, there are certain factors to be kept in mind. Some of these factors are as follows:

1. No arrangement of flowers, containers, pedestals, potted plants, or candelabras should be placed where they will interfere with any portion of the service, obstruct the view of anyone in the congregation, or hamper the movement of the people in the church at any time.

2. The flowers should not be at the altar rail if communion is to be served.

3. The flower arrangement should be bold and distinct, not feathery. People in the congregation should be able to distinguish the flowers in the arrangement instead of having to wonder what flowers are being used. The arrangement must not distract the worshippers.

4. The flower arrangement should be easily viewed from the back of the church. It should be visible to all. The arrangement must be so designed that it is artistically complete from all angles. It should be in scale with the church.

5. The designer should follow the procedures of the church and place the arrangement in the proper place.

6. No part of the flower and foliages should be in front of the cross.

7. The container must blend in with the flowers, foliages, and structure of the church. Some beautiful containers are completely out of place in some churches. A white container with no white flowers in the arrangement would "stand out like a sore thumb" and attract too much attention to the flower arrangement.

8. The container should have a firm base so that it will not only appear steady and secure, but must also be weighty enough to hold a large arrangement of flowers and plant materials without falling over.

part
VI

FLOWERS
FOR PERSONAL
ADORNMENT

20

Flowers to Wear

People, particularly women, have worn flowers for personal adornment since the dawn of civilization. Fresh flowers and foliages have been used to embellish the hair, wrist, knee, and ankle, or as a clothing accent at the shoulder, neckline, and waist. Flowers increase the wearers' charm and lift their spirits. The creation of corsages, garlands, bracelets, and hair decorations requires knowledge and use of the same principles of design, balance, scale, harmony, and focal point as are used for other arrangements.

Corsage making is not only a pleasant and rewarding experience, but can save money. One's own garden can supply the materials in season. A few flowers can be purchased from the local florist when outdoor flowers are not available for a corsage, or flowers from a flower arrangement or potted plant in the home may be used.

Corsages for afternoon wear are casual (as is the attire); they are generally smaller and have little or no ribbon compared to corsages worn for evening events. Flowers should match the formality of the occasion. For example, orchids, carnations, and roses are appropriate for formal wear, while coarse-textured, common garden-type flowers are best for informal wear.

CORSAGES

Supplies and Materials

A corsage requires some supplies; without them it is virtually impossible to make a clever and "professional looking" corsage. The materials which will be needed, in addition to the flowers and possibly some foliage, are: a sharp knife and/or shears capable of cutting soft wire, cut florists' wire, floral stem wrap (sold under the trade name of Floratape) in several colors, or at least green and white, colored pipe stem cleaners, several colors of narrow (⅓ to ⅝ inch) ribbon, artificial wired leaves, tulle (fine nylon net), spools of heavy green thread or plastic-coated wire (sold under the trade name of Pigtail), ribbon scissors, and corsage pins.

The designer florists' wire is available in gauges 20, 22, 24, 26, and 30. The size and weight of the flower head will determine which gauge to use. Flowers are wired with artificial stems to reduce bulk by removing the natural stem to reduce weight, for greater comfort of the wearer, for ease in making the flowers face the correct way, and to keep flowers in place if they begin to wilt (Figure 20.1).

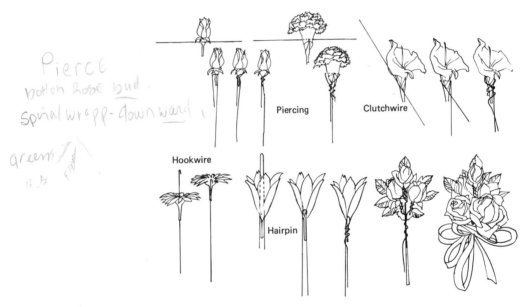

Figure 20.1 Types of wiring flowers for a corsage. (Courtesy Pennsylvania State University.)

A knife is best for cutting flowers but shears may also be used.

The stem wrap is used to cover the wired artificial stems. A colored pipe stem, usually green, may sometimes be used as artificial stems by pushing it up into the calyx of some flowers such as roses and carnations for a quick nontaping job.

The ribbon is used to add a bow for additional accent and focus and sometimes to "finish" the stems of the completed corsage (Figure 20.2). Rib-

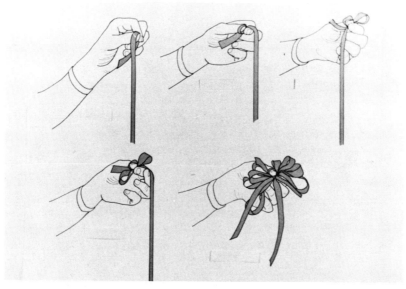

Figure 20.2 Steps in tying a bow of ribbon for a corsage. (Courtesy Pennsylvania State University.)

bon suitable for corsages comes in three usable widths: #1 (⅜ inch), #2 (½ inch), and #3 (⅝ inch).

Since natural foliage often does not stay fresh and crisp long enough to be used, artificial satin or velvet leaves are used to make a professional-looking and attractive corsage.

The green thread and plastic-coated wire may be used for tying certain flowers together. The plastic-coated wire can also be used to hold a ribbon bow together and to fasten the bow into the corsage.

The wire, floral stem wrap, artificial leaves, corsage pins, and plastic-coated wire usually can be obtained from a local florist. Wholesale supply houses only do business with the retail florist. Garden clubs sometimes have a person who supplies corsage materials to club members.

If several corsages are to be constructed, the designer might consider making a corsage cabinet, as shown in Figure 20.3. Then everything needed to make corsages will be right at the designer's fingertips.

The use of large bows and gobs of artificial leaves and tulle is definitely old-fashioned. Today's corsages have a neat, natural, restrained look.

Flowers and Foliages for Corsages

Only certain garden flowers are durable enough to be used in corsages and even these may not last longer than one day. Therefore, it is essential to use the flowers the same day they are cut. Be sure to cut both buds and open

Figure 20.3 A corsage cabinet set up for easy construction of a corsage. (Courtesy Pennsylvania State University.)

flowers. They should be cut in the early morning or in the late afternoon and properly hardened by placing the stems in deep cans of warm water (100 to 110°F) and allowing them to stand in a cool place for several hours.

Garden flowers that make good corsages and will hold up for the evening are: rose, *camellia*, carnation, sweet William, *spirea*, aster, chrysanthemum, cornflower, daisy, *gaillardia*, canterbury bell, *zinnia*, and individual florets of *delphinium*, snapdragon, and *gladiolus*. Daylilies make an attractive corsage but can only be used in the daytime. At the Christmas season, corsages are made of evergreens, including holly, pine cones, and berries. They look very attractive on coats.

Florists usually have roses, carnations, pompon chrysanthemums, orchids, *gladiolus*, and gardenias available the year round for corsages. Seasonally, the florist may have *camellias*, Dutch iris, daffodils, tulips, and asters.

Foliage which can be used in corsages includes most evergreens, *camellia*, gardenia, leatherleaf fern, croton, magnolia, iris, *gladiolus*, dusty miller, asparagus, privet, and others. Use the foliage belonging to the flowers in the corsage if it is the right size and resists wilting. Rose foliage is useless since it wilts too quickly.

Buds and small flowers are placed at the top or outer edges of any corsage; larger open flowers belong at the base or center, as when arranging flowers in containers.

Places to Wear Corsages

There are four places on the body where corsages are commonly worn, and a special type for each location. A shoulder corsage may be triangular, shield-shaped, or a style that complements the clothing of the wearer with the ribbon usually at or near the bottom (Figures 20.4 and 20.5). Waist and wrist corsages are frequently double corsages made by constructing two small triangular corsages and tying them together base to base with the ribbon in the center. A hair corsage takes various shapes but is usually made without the use of foliage and either with or without a ribbon bow.

Constructing the Shoulder Corsage

To construct a shoulder corsage, start with a leaf and bud at the top followed by two small flowers. Foliage or accessories such as tulle, ribbon loops, and so forth, are added along the way. Tie the first two flowers and bud together firmly with a pipe cleaner, thread, or 26-gauge wire. Any method of fastening the stems together is satisfactory. Turn the flower heads to the front. Add most of the foliage and one flower at a time, making sure to tie or wire each firmly to the others with a pipe cleaner, thread, or the wire stem. Cut off all long stems and add a small bow of ribbon at the base. Be sure this is placed snugly under the last flower so there is no gap, and make it small enough so it does not detract from the flowers. The completed shoulder corsage should resemble the ones shown in Figure 20.4 and 20.5.

Figure 20.4 A rose shoulder corsage. (Courtesy Pennsylvania State University.)

Figure 20.5 A shoulder corsage of two *cymbidium* orchids. (Courtesy Pennsylvania State University.)

Wear the corsage with the flowers, not stems, upright—the way they grow in nature.

Some corsages can be made without wire. Flowers which have a lightweight stem and do not wilt easily (such as lady slipper orchids), may be held together with strong thread in a triangular design. The stems should stick out irregularly; a bow of ribbon may or may not be used. This makes a very attractive informal corsage.

The Mechanics of Wiring and Florataping Flowers and Foliages

When the flowers are properly hardened, you are ready to begin. The first step is to remove the stems of the flowers, leaving just ½ inch on the flower. The flowers are then ready for wiring. The gauge of wire used will depend on the size and weight of the flower head. We usually use #22 or #24 gauge wire on outdoor roses since they are fairly heavy. There are four methods of wiring flowers (see Figure 20.1). The method chosen will depend on the type of flower. The piercing method is used on roses and carnations, the clutch wire on *gladiolus* florets, the hairpin on individual hyacinth florets and daylilies, and the hookwire method on aster and daisy-type flowers. The important thing is to provide a good, substantial artificial stem for the flowers.

The wire should next be wrapped with green or white floratape. Hold the floratape in the right hand and the flower in the left. Stretch the tape and twist the wire. As the flower is rotated, the floratape is guided and stretched around the wire, starting at the flower head and working down the stem. Hands should be kept dry when wrapping the stem. Floratape is not sticky in itself but it clings to the wire from the pressure of the winding.

Tying A Ribbon Bow

Most corsages are enhanced by a small attractive bow of ribbon which gives them a "finished" look. It takes about one and a half yards of regular narrow ribbon for each corsage. Choose a color that will harmonize with the flowers and not detract from them. One way of tying a bow is as follows:

1. Hang the ribbon over your left thumb with the long side in front and about 2 inches behind, as shown in Figure 20.2.

2. With your right hand, take the long side of the ribbon and loop it under and around the left thumb, squeezing the ribbon between the left thumb and forefinger.

3. Grasp the ribbon with the right hand about 3 inches from the crushed part and make a loop in the air, bringing the ribbon to the spot between the left thumb and forefinger and crushing it between the two. The ribbon must always be looped "under" so the ribbon will fit between the left thumb and forefinger. Never leave the ribbon flat, but crush it after each loop. Looping over instead of under will make bow tying more difficult.

4. Go down the ribbon 3 inches and loop it up under, crushing again between the left thumb and forefinger. We have created our first two loops.

5. Three or four more loops are made in each direction until the bow reaches the proper size. Each set of loops should be slightly larger than the previous set so the bow will have more character and not look artificial.

6. Cut another piece of ribbon about 8 inches long. Insert this under the first small loop in place of your left thumb and by pulling it down on both sides, tie it at the back. This will hold the bow as you have constructed it.

7. Using the two ends of the short piece with which you tied the bow together, fasten the bow to the corsage snugly against the bottom flower and tie securely with the short ribbon ends. (A piece of #30 wire wrapped with floratape can also be used to hold the bow onto the corsage.)

8. Trim off any ribbon ends that seem too long, and the corsage is finished. Don't forget a corsage pin to hold it to the dress.

For a wrist corsage, use a special wristlet and fasten the corsage securely to it. A wristlet frame may be made out of taped wire, pipe stem cleaners, or purchased from the florist with an elastic band and aluminum fastener. The plastic circle on the interior of a roll of floratape can be cut and taped for an inexpensive and permanent wristlet band.

BOUTONNIERES

Boutonnieres are flowers that are worn on the shoulder or lapel of a suit. A boutonniere is just one flower wired exactly as it would be in a corsage, and wrapped with floratape. An informal boutonniere is just a plain flower, whereas a formal boutonniere has a piece of green attached behind the flower and held in place with floratape. A boutonniere pin should also be supplied. Usually there is no ribbon with a boutonniere; however, this seems to be changing in today's fashion. Boutonnieres may be worn by men or women.

part
VII

FLOWER COMPETITION AND JUDGING

21

Competitive
Flower Arranging

Preparing arrangements for competition in a flower show is not for everyone. Competitive flower arranging is for those individuals who enjoy this extra challenge. When flower artists make an arrangement for the home, they need only please themselves and guests, if any. Criticism is unlikely. But the arranger who enters a competition must be prepared for tension, criticism, and disappointment. It can also be exciting and enjoyable.

The arranger must strive to create a flower arrangement that will please judges, who are likely to have rigorous standards. A competitor must have the strength to accept criticism and the desire to do better.

The necessary effort and type of personality to compete in a flower arranging show has been especially well expressed by Mrs. C. G. Scholz in her article, "All the Arts in Flower Arrangement":

> Have you ever considered just what a flower arranger must do to exhibit in a big show? We will suppose that she has studied the schedule, made her entry and has formed some idea of the picture she wishes to create. She must decide on a container that she possesses, or buy, borrow, or make one. Weeks before the show she must line up the material that will be available at the time to exhibit and start days before to collect. If she isn't growing it herself she will need all her persuasive powers to get the florist to cut buds and long stems, take the material home to harden it overnight, get up at dawn on the day of the show to pack everything so as to get an early start, sometimes needing the strength of an Amazon to carry heavy containers and material. She rushes to the place of exhibit and upon arriving tries to look calm and collected, while contacting the entry chairman, all the time deeply concerned about the condition of her

flowers, for which she has hunted up hill and down dale, through swampy places and in deep woods. After she is assigned her working space, which at times is quite limited, she is ready to design her flowers, rubbing elbows with half a dozen temperamental artists all in the same boat as she. She must work with the precision of a watch to get the arrangement in its allotted space on time, hoping that it will stand up at least until the judges see it. If she wins one of the honors, all is well, but if she loses she must accept adverse decisions cheerfully and, with the grace of a diplomat, congratulate the winners. While quickly recovering herself, she looks around for the schedule of the next flower show. Flower arrangers are a hardy race of women! My advice to all is, exhibit as often as possible, for the day is not very far off when we will be glad to pay for the privilege of exhibiting in a flower show just as the painter and sculptor pay to have their works exhibited. The new art of flower arrangement is growing by leaps and bounds, and soon there will be so many exhibitors that our work will have to pass a jury before it is admitted to a show.[1]

PREPARATION FOR COMPETITIVE ARRANGEMENTS

The flower arranger must check the flower show schedule carefully and decide what is necessary in a specific show class to win a blue ribbon. The specifications for the types of classes should be read carefully. When designing a flower arrangement for entry into a flower show for competitive purposes, be sure to select the right class for entering the arrangement. The general rules are set forth in the program and must be followed exactly. Note when accessories may or may not be used. The schedule may list a glossary so that the judges and the designers will know what is meant by the flower show committee. The glossary refers to those terms used in the descriptive titles of the various judging class categories of the point scale system of judging. Some are:

Arrangement: Plant material organized in a design which follows recognized artistic principles.

Balance: Placement of elements to create equilibrium; both actual and visual weight.

Color: The use of hue, value, and chroma in harmonious relationships and serving a purpose in the design.

Composition: A planned design of plant material, container, and base; may also include background fabric, accessories, setting, and use.

Condition: The physical condition of the plant materials used. An indication of the grower's or arranger's skill in producing, selecting,

[1] Mrs. C. G. Scholz, "All the Arts in Flower Arrangement," *Bulletin of the National Council of State Garden Clubs, Incorporated,* Vol. XVII, Nos. 4-5, April-May (1946).

using, and handling of plant materials. Half dead or wilted flowers will count down heavily on the arrangement.

Design: Visual elements organized and arranged in an artistic manner to make a pleasing whole.

Distinction: Superiority achieved through craftmanship, inspiration, and proficiency. It includes beauty, originality, and creativity.

Harmony: Aesthetic value when the composition has orderly, consistent, or a pleasing arrangement of parts. The lack of discordant parts.

Originality: The conception or plan behind the design. Often it is an unusual or different combination of plant materials, containers, and/or accessories used together.

Relation to container: Includes consideration of the scale, color, texture, and general character of the plant material in relation to the container.

Scale: The actual and apparent size relationship of the components of the arrangement.

Suitability: Appropriate relationship of parts.

Texture: The visual quality of the surface structure.

After carefully reading the schedule and deciding what class or classes to compete in, the next step is to get an *idea* for the arrangement. Determine if the arrangement is to be interpretive (expressive) or decorative. Then roughly sketch the design idea on paper. Do not try to include all the details but rough out the main lines, center of interest, and the container shape. Rework the sketch until you are satisfied that all the principles of good design—scale, unity, accent, harmony, balance, repetition, and rhythm— have been included. At this point, the designer might resort to crayons, colored chalk, colored pencils, or felt pens to work out the color harmony.

Next choose the flowers and foliages that will be available. Sometimes it will be necessary to consider what plant materials will be available before working out a plan.

A few days before the show, make a "dry run" of the arrangement. After completing it, try to evaluate the arrangement objectively, using the official scale of points. If possible, ask a friend who is also a good flower arranger to criticize the arrangement. At this point, improvements can be made. The day of the show is too late to try modifications.

When satisfied, prepare a checklist of materials. The list should include not only the planter materials, containers, and accessories, but also all the tools and supplies needed.

On the day of the show, arrive early. Frequently, working space is very limited and it is a matter of first come, first served. Get an area "tied down" early, try for good light and adequate space. Work diligently and intelli-

Figure 21.1 A vertical arrangement of spring flowers for competition in a garden flower show. (Courtesy Pennsylvania State University.)

gently, do not waste valuable time fussing about details that have minimum value. Work hardest on the details that have the most value. The composition must be finished on time (Figure 21.1).

Most flower arranging judges are well qualified. A visit with them after the show may be a valuable way to gather tips and pointers for the next competition.

SUGGESTED SCALE OF POINTS FOR JUDGING

Most judging of flower arrangements and horticultural specimens is done with a point scale of 100 points. However, unless the judges have actually been asked to do exact point scoring, they judge visually, keeping the point score in their minds and comparing arrangements with a theoretical, perfect arrangement of a similar type. There are many sets of judging points for specific types of flower arrangements. The main ones are listed in Table 21-1.

Many judges will use a variation of these suggested points. An accredited

Table 21-1 *Point scale for flower arrangements*

Type of arrangement	Point scale
Flower arranging without a definite design, color harmony, suitability to placement, or occasion being named:	
Design	30
Color harmony	20
Distinction and originality	20
Relation to container	10
Suitability of combination of materials	10
Condition	10
	100
Flower arrangements for a coffee table:	
Design	20
Color harmony	20
Distinction and originality	20
Suitability to occasion	15
Relation to container	10
Suitability of combination	5
Condition	10
	100
Table centerpieces:	
Color harmony	20
Distinction and originality	20
Perfection of centerpiece	20
Relationship of textures	10
Proportion and balance of accessories	10
Suitability to occasion	10
Condition	10
	100
Table arrangements for a buffet supper:	
Distinction and originality	40
Suitability of combination of material	20
Color harmony	15
Proportion and balance	15
Condition	10
	100
Traditional occidental period arrangements:	
Period correctness	25
Design correctness	25
Color suitability	20
Appropriate materials and container	20
Condition	10
	100

Table 21-1 con't

Japanese traditional arrangements:

Design correctness according to style	40
Style correctness	20
Suitability of materials, container, base, and accessories	20
Distinction	10
Condition	10
	100

Line arrangements:

Design	25
Simplicity	25
Suitability to occasion	20
Color harmony	15
Suitability of combination	10
Condition	5
	100

Line-mass arrangements:

Design	30
Color harmony	30
Distinction	20
Relation to container	10
Condition	10
	100

Miniatures (in miniatures, the most important principle is scale. A regular miniature is under 5 inches overall, and a dwarf miniature is under 3 inches overall):

Scale	40
Design	30
Color harmony	15
Individuality	10
Condition, suitability	5
	100

Fruit or vegetable arrangements with or without flowers:

Color harmony	35
Distinction and originality	20
Proportion and balance	15
Suitability to occasion	10
Relation to container	10
Condition	10
	100

Table 21-1 con't

Corsages:

Design and color	35
Distinction and originality	20
Technique	15
Suitability to occasion	10
Combination of materials	10
Condition	10
	100

Niches, shadow boxes, and flower pictures (arrangements in special settings of specified size with perhaps a greater emphasis on proportion and scale, use of accessories, textual harmonies, effects of lighting, and value of shadows. The space relationship between the arrangement and the niche must be just right. The niche should be neither too large nor too small):

Scale and proportion: relation of all materials to space and to each other	30
Design: relationship of line, mass, balance, and accent	25
Color harmony	15
Distinction and originality	10
Suitability of materials and accessories	10
Condition	10
	100

Bouquets, vases, and baskets of flowers (flowers displayed in the above containers usually require less artistic treatment but design cannot be completely ignored. Reflects a greater need for color, condition, and appropriateness):

Condition	30
Color	25
Arrangement	20
Suitability of purpose	15
Distinction and originality	10
	100

Collections (collections are more concerned with the number of kinds and varieties gathered together):

Diversity: kinds and varieties	35
Arrangement and design	25
Quality and condition	25
Educational value (proper labeling)	15
	100

Displays (displays have emphasis on attractiveness of the arrangement of the materials grown for perfection):

Arrangement and design	40
Quality and condition	35
Number and kinds of varieties	15
Educational value (proper labeling)	10
	100

judge may follow the point scale found in the *Handbook for Flower Shows,* 1977 edition from the National Council of State Garden Clubs, Inc. (Table 21-2). Certain plant societies have their own scale of points for judging a given specific plant. It may be used at the discretion of the show chairman and will be indicated in the program.

Table 21-2 *Point scales for judging horticultural classes*

Horticultural classes	Point scale
Cut flowers (applicable to all varieties):	
Cultural perfection (60 pts. total)	
Form, color, substance, floriferousness	20
Size (scale)	20
Foliage and stem	20
Distinction of species	20
Condition	20
	100
Flowering potted plants:	
Cultural perfection	35
Size of plant	20
Floriferousness	15
Rarity	10
Color	10
Foliage	10
	100
Foliage potted plants:	
Cultural perfection	35
Size of plant	20
Distinction	15
Rarity	15
Form	15
	100
Collection of cut flowers:	
Cultural perfection	45
Type and variety	30
Staging	20
Correct labeling	5
	100

SUGGESTED INTERPRETIVE CLASSES FOR A FLOWER SHOW

Many flower arranging shows will have a list of competitive classes built around a central theme. The theme is frequently determined by the season of the year; for example, "Fall Harvest," "Spring's Song," "Prelude to Summer," "Winter Interlude," "Christmas Bells," "Summer Magic," "Songs of the Sea," "Mountain Freshness," etc. The class titles then relate directly to the theme. However, at other times the class titles may just be very general and not too restrictive, as for instance, a naturalistic (balance) arrangement in a vase or a one-flower arrangement using only one flower (no buds or flower clusters) with foliage and/or accessories.

Here are some examples of interpretive class titles from actual flower shows:

Title	Description
The Golden Triangle	Design interpreting the Golden Triangle in Pittsburgh. Niche 34″ × 24″ × 20″.
Along the Lake Shore	Composition using driftwood. Niche 34″ × 24″ × 20″.
The Poconos	An all-white arrangement using a minimum of foliage.
Colonial Breakfast Table	A flower arrangement for a breakfast table, cardtable size. Linens and one-place setting to be provided by the exhibitor.
Lilliputian Village	A miniature arrangement not exceeding three inches overall.
"A Tisket, A Tasket"	An arrangement in a wicker or reed basket, using wild flowers.
September Song	A brown and green arrangement combining fresh and dried material, and using an accessory(ies).
Books and Blossoms	"Cheaper By the Dozen" (Gilbraith). Arrangement of twelve blossoms of one kind of flower and one color.
"Rube Goldberg"	Abstract. Names of flowering plants using inanimate objects.
Lavender and Old Lace	Arrangement of old-fashioned garden flowers and an accessory of lace.
Fall Weekend	An arrangement of autumn flowers and foliages for a guestroom desk or dressing table.

The designer should make sure the flower arrangement will fit in with the title of the class as well as following the suggestions in the description. The judge will consider both of these in reaching a decision.

JUDGING PROCEDURES

"He that judges without informing himself to the utmost that he is capable, cannot acquit himself for judging amiss." John Locke (1632-1704).

When a flower show is being staged by a garden club affiliated with the National Council of State Garden Clubs, Inc., the show must be organized and conducted strictly according to requirements set forth in the latest edition of the *Handbook for Flower Shows.* The sanctioned flower show will then be eligible for national competition. Accredited and student judges who judge at the show may use this experience toward gaining their judges certificate.

There are four levels of certification for National Council Flower Show judges: (1) student judge; (2) accredited flower show judge; (3) life judge; and (4) master judge. First place award winners in a sanctioned show may also use this for accreditation of judging certificates. The blue ribbons needed are for horticulture and design.

The ribbons awarded by the judges in an accredited flower show are blue for first place, red for second, yellow for third, and white, if there are to be any, for honorable mention places. Ribbons are given in each class to be judged. However, this does not mean that there will always be a blue, red, and yellow. In fact, if there is only *one* entry in a class, it may not get a blue ribbon. It is up to the judges to evaluate the single entry on its own merit, based on a perfect arrangement in the mind's eye of the judge.

Some flower shows are not accredited by the National Council so that they may draw up their own rules and regulations. In this situation, it is possible to award more than one blue, red, or yellow ribbon in each class. This is not possible in a "standard show" of the National Council where no more than one ribbon can be awarded unless it is an honorable mention.

Arrangers indicate how high they have set their goals by which shows they enter. The National Council of State Garden Clubs, Inc., sets a very high standard of excellence, and their shows are recognized for their high quality.

Judges who have agreed to serve should be sure to get there on time and should be familiar with the schedule of classes. The judge should look over the whole show to get an overall picture of the types of arrangements that are exhibited. The judge should discuss the show and procedures with the show committee. Usually judge(s) will be stricter and more demanding when judging a show sponsored by an older established garden club, and more lenient when judging the entries in a newly formed club. Standards will be relaxed a little so as not to discourage the members of a newly formed garden club holding its first or second flower show.

The judge should make a quick survey of all the entries in a class and eliminate those from consideration that do not come up to standard and will not have a chance of winning a ribbon. The judging is a process of elimination down to the top three or four entries. Judges should not hesitate to discuss their decisions with the members of the garden club after the judging is over.

part
VIII

FLOWER ARRANGING IN THE FUTURE

22

The Future of Flower Arranging

American flower arranging is a comparatively young art. It really only began in its own right about 1900. Until recently, flower arranging existed in the shadow of the classical arts, especially painting and sculpture. Now it is no longer considered a passing fad but is recognized as an art form in its own right.

Flower arranging differs from other arts in that it has its own media; arrangers grow their own materials. The plants themselves possess beauty and harmony from nature. From this preorganized material, we select or reject it according to the elements and principles of design. We use the color as provided by nature and change or enhance it by combining it with others.

Plant material can be used conventionally or abstractly. The American line–mass flower arrangements in this book are generally considered conventional. The line is taken from the Japanese three-lined arrangements, and the mass and color from European designs. The designer may progress to newer designs which may be labeled modernistic or even futuristic. Currently this represents unbroken ground where form, style, and imagination have no limits. Perhaps nontraditional and abstract arrangements are more appropriate for modern homes. These arrangements can be seen most frequently at flower shows where individual creativity is stressed. An arrangement may be labeled as a certain style after its completion. The arranger may not have intended the arrangement to fit a particular category but was merely following his or her creative instincts.

The trend in recent years has been away from the stylized forms of

Figure 22.1 *Elongated Beauty.* (Courtesy Mrs. Michael Thomas, Sacramento, CA.)

arrangements such as the symmetrical triangle, asymmetrical triangle, horizontal, and others of the 13 geometric forms. These time-proven standard forms are still seen and are appropriate for most occasions. "Flowers by wire" will surely continue to conform to the usual patterns for many years. Free-form styles of flower arrangements may become more common in American houses with time.

The use of artichoke blossoms, *aralia* leaves and twisted wisteria curved around in front of a dried palm spatha in a tall cylindrical container in Figure 22.1 is an attractive example of the free-form style of flower arranging.

CONTEMPORARY FLOWER DESIGN CATEGORIES

Nontraditional, 20th-century flower arranging styles can be arbitrarily divided into two types, based on the method of construction. *Radial structure* is based on the idea that the structured area radiates from a strong or subtle area of interest at or near the single point of emergence, with interest tapering to the outer edges. This includes the Traditional (Conventional), Modern, Free Style, and the 'Isms (Impressionism, Cubism, etc.) styles.

The *interest-equated style* has the emphasis spread over the whole arrangement, with no single point of emergence required or focal area emphasized. This style category includes Abstracts, Mobiles, Avant-Garde, Progressive Art, and Abstract 'Isms designs.

RADIAL DESIGNS

The radial designs were, in general, the first styles to break away from the traditional type. An early variation of the traditional design was the naturalistic style. In this style, the designer portrays the natural growth habit of the particular plant material being used. For example, the composition may consist of one or more stems of German iris with the largest flower up high, emerging from a fan-shaped cluster of their own leaves.

A more recent type of radial design is the free-form or free-style design. A free-form arrangement uses easily flowing lines or natural curves having variation of direction or change of direction and outlines, rather than straight lines, sharp angles, and precise curves. The designs are created outside the basic geometric patterns of the past, such as triangles and circles, etc. M. "Buddy" Benz, in his book, *Flowers: Free Form—Interpretive Designs,* has this to say about free-form designs:

> Free Form–Interpretive Design is pure design in the true sense of the word. It has independent personality that is appreciated for itself. It is timeless—it is not dated—as is shown in the works of art from the Grecian, Etruscan, and Roman periods that are used today in contemporary designs. Its intrinsic value is found in the aesthetic beauty created ... Free Form in design means unshackled imagination, guided by principles, free of tradition and man-made rules ... The new concept of floral design is influenced by space-form cutting its own design in atmosphere.[1]

Modern designs have tended toward more stylized variations of the free form and tend toward abstraction. They overlap and may be modern or abstract in concept and/or construction. Ultramodern designs are more of a free-style arrangement without sticking strictly to various "suggested rules" and regulations used by the beginner. These are what are termed creative designs in which the flower arranger creates a floral arrangement or design for a particular occasion, setting, or mood.

[1]M. Benz, *Flowers: Free Form—Interpretive Designs,* Houston, Texas: San Jacinto Publishing Co., 1960, p.154.

INTEREST-EQUATED DESIGNS

The interest-equated styles of design are the newest feature of floral art and will probably gain more attention in the future. One type is the abstract collage, an arrangement—usually framed—created by gluing a combination of diverse, often unrelated, fragments and objects to a surface to emphasize texture and three-dimensional effects. It may be expressive or nonobjective. It is generally made to be hung.

A variation of the collage is the assemblage, the fitting together, in an aesthetically pleasing manner, of parts and pieces of machinery, scrap, "found" items, wood, stone, possessions, and plant materials. The result may be two-dimensional or three-dimensional. Both collage and assemblage generally use "throwaways," artifacts, and "found" items.

"Avant-garde," the newest trend, differs from assemblage in positions, concepts, and in that it incorporates "ready-mades," unused, the unmarked rather than "throwaways" and artifacts. Avant-garde is the use of original,

Figure 22.2 *Fantastique.* [See also Color Plate.] (Courtesy Mrs. H. E. Brown, Ozona, FL.)

unconventional design ideas, materials, and techniques. Space and movement are emphasized as in all abstracts. The design uses plant materials with the wood, plastic, steel, etc., or the design becomes foreign to our medium.

Mobiles recently began incorporating flower design. Mobiles are a composition of suspended balanced moving parts. They involve action stressed with space and may be constructed from all manner of objects and materials. As Buddy Benz suggests by "space-form cutting its own design in atmosphere," we can visualize movement through the construction and use of mobiles in flower arranging. Dried materials as well as small fresh flowers in a foam can be used in a flower arrangement in motion.

An interpretive design *(Fantastique)* is well illustrated in Figure 22.2. This floral interpretation of the Hector Berlioz Symphonies uses pink *anthuriums,* philodendron, and bleached willow in a very modern design using a fantasy musical note cut out of spray-painted styrofoam.

WHAT OF THE FUTURE?

Traditional (conventional) designs will not, in the foreseeable future, disappear from the American flower arranging scene. The elements and principles of design for all art forms are so ingrained and valuable that they never will be lost. But there are those creative souls who will want to add a new dimension of experience to their repertoire. Therefore, we predict that the future of American flower arranging lies in a turning more toward a free style and eventually to abstract designs while still adhering to the fundamental principles of art. There will be different forms of abstract art depending upon how far from the "normal" the designer wishes to go. The flower arranger will not likely achieve total abstraction as is found in some of our modern paintings and sculptures. The trend is to place more emphasis on the whole composition and less on just the material and containers. Abstract containers as well as abstract accessories will play a larger part in the composition of American flower arrangements of the future.

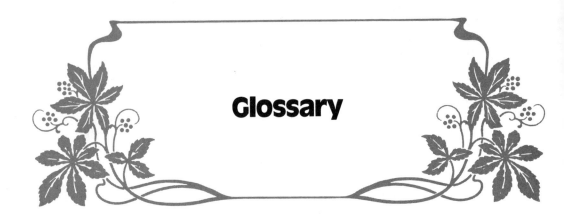

Glossary

Abstract Design: A creative art form using space along with line, form, color, and texture to create the flower arrangement by using plant material and other components.

Accent: Emphasis, importance.

Accessory: Any object in a composition in addition to plant material, container, base, background, or mechanics, which is supplemental to the theme.

Advancing Colors: Warm hues from red to yellow.

Analogous Color Harmony: Two or three colors adjacent to each other on the color wheel.

Arrangement: Plant material organized in a container or on a base in accordance with recognized art principles.

Artificial: Manufactured to simulate natural appearances.

Asymmetrical Balance: Two sides of a vertical axis in an arrangement that are different in composition but equal in *visual* weight.

Background: The surface behind and under a composition against which it is viewed.

Balance: Placement of materials to achieve visual stability.

Base: A component under the container.

Bonsai: A plant material (tree) trained to a particular form in miniature.

Bract: A modified leaf often colored and mistaken for a flower petal such as in a poinsettia.

220

Chroma: The intensity of a color or hue.

Color: Visual response of the eye to reflected light. A design element.

Complementary Colors: Colors exactly opposite each other on the color wheel.

Composition: A planned design of plant material, container, base, and use; it may also include background fabric, accessories, and setting.

Condition: The physical state of the plant materials used. An indication of the grower's or designer's skill in producing, using, handling, and selecting plant materials.

Container: Any receptacle which holds plant materials—fresh, dried, or artificial.

Cool Colors: Blues, greens, and white.

Della Robbia Wreath: A circle of greens decorated with fruits, nuts, cones, seed pods, or berries typical of the Renaissance period.

Design: Overall form of the arrangement. A planned relationship of flowers, foliages, container, and background.

Dish Garden: A miniature landscape of small plants planted in soil in a low pottery container.

Distinction: Superiority achieved through craftsmanship, inspiration, and proficiency; it entails beauty, originality, and shows the result of uninhibited creative effort.

Dominance: A strong compelling effect of one or more elements of design.

Dried Material: Natural plant material which has been preserved by the removal of moisture.

Driftwood: Wood that has been water-washed.

Floret: A small, individual flower of an inflorescence.

Flower Arranging: The art of placing floral material in a container in a pleasing manner following various artistic principles.

Foliage: The leaves of a plant, shrub, or tree.

Forcing: Bringing plants into bloom at a time other than normal in nature.

Form: Shape and outline of the design. The habit of growth of plant materials which is a design element.

Formal: Regular and conventional, symmetrical.

Free-form Design: A new concept in creative art form free from conventional ideas and patterns; nongeometric.

Free Standing: An all-around arrangement to be viewed from all sides.

Gradation: Gradual change in size, form, color, or texture.

Harmony: Aesthetic value when the composition possesses an orderly, consistent, or pleasing arrangement of parts; the lack of discordant parts.

Horticulture: The science of producing, improving, storing, and marketing flowers, fruits, ornamentals, and vegetables.

Hue: The colors of the spectrum; the name of a color.

Inflorescence: The particular arrangement of the parts of a flower.

Informal: Casual or free and easy; in balance—naturalistic, asymmetrical.

Intensity: The brightness or dullness of a color.

Line: A design element. A continuous visual path. An extension of a point.

Linear Form: A geometric outline of the composition.

Miniature: A small arrangement 5 inches or less overall (in every direction; 3 inches or less overall for a dwarf miniature.

Monochromatic Color Harmony: Tints, tones, and shades of one hue.

Naturalistic: Using plant material as it grows to represent an actual scene.

Neutral Colors: White, black, and gray.

Niche: A recessed or open-front box to display a flower arrangement.

Nosegay: A tight hand bouquet of fragrant flowers.

Novelty: A container of unusual form or shape such as a heart, animal, etc.

Originality: The product of one's thoughts and imagination. Independent, not copied.

Pattern: Silhouette of a composition using voids and spaces for part of the design.

Period Arrangement: Relating to a definite era in European history.

Primary Colors: Red, yellow, and blue.

Repetition: The repeating of one or more components in an arrangement.

Rhythm: A graceful, visual effect that suggests movement. A principle of design.

Scale: The actual and visual size relationship of the component parts (of the arrangement).

Secondary Colors: Orange, green, and violet.

Shades: A hue plus black.

Silhouette: The outline of an arrangement against its background; pattern.

Space: The open areas in and around the arrangement; a design element.

Spike: An elongated flower with florets all along the upper stem.

Spray: A flower with side branches and blooms on all sides.

Suitability: Appropriate relationship of parts.

Symmetrical Balance: The two sides of a vertical axis that appear as though they are the same (also conventional).

Terrarium: A garden of small plants in an enclosed glass container.

Tertiary Colors: Combination of a primary and secondary color, such as blue-green or orange-red.

Texture: The quality of the surface structure. A design element.

Tint: A hue with white added.

Tone: A hue with gray added.

Tussy Mussy: A circle of small flowers arranged around one central flower similar to a nosegay.

Unity: A principle of design; the pleasant aesthetic effect achieved when all parts and elements that make up a composition appear to go well together.

Value of Color: The lightness or darkness of a color.

Voids: Spaces in a composition open at the margin of the design, but not holes.

Warm Colors: Advancing colors of red through yellow.

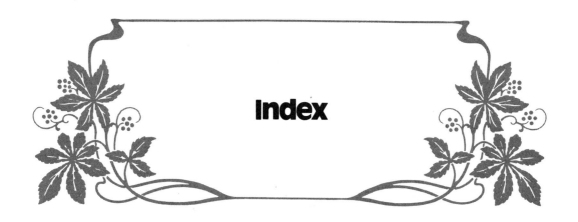

Index